Numeracy Pupil's Book

Year 5

Peter Patilla &
Paul Broadbent

Every effort has been made to trace copyright holders and to obtain their permission for the use of copyright material. The authors and publishers will gladly receive information enabling them to rectify any error or omission in subsequent editions.

First published 1999

Letts Educational, Schools and Colleges Division, 9–15 Aldine Street, London W12 8AW
Tel: (020) 8740 2270
Fax: (020) 8740 2280

Text © Peter Patilla and Paul Broadbent
Editorial, design and production © Gecko Limited, Bicester, Oxon
Illustrations © Peter and Janet Simmonett, except Beccy Blake: p. 42, 76; Jan Nesbitt: pp. 38, 78; David Pattison: pp. 28, 64; Andy Warrington: pp. 16, 40.
Cover illustration © Beccy Blake.

British Library Cataloguing-in-Publication Data
A CIP record for this book is available from the British Library.

ISBN 1 84085 275 5
Printed and bound in Spain
Letts Educational is the trading name of BPP [Letts Educational] Ltd

CONTENTS

Do you remember?

1 What does this number say?

8050

- **a** eight hundred and fifty
- **b** eight thousand and fifty
- **c** eight thousand and five
- **d** eighty thousand and fifty

2 How many pennies?

- **a** 105
- **b** 1005
- **c** 1500
- **d** 1050

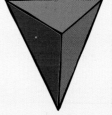
£10.05

3 How many millimetres?

- **a** 75
- **b** 7500
- **c** 250
- **d** 750

$\frac{3}{4}$ **metre**

4 Name the shape.

- **a** prism
- **b** tetrahedron
- **c** heptagon
- **d** icosahedron

5 Name the triangle.

- **a** equilateral
- **b** scalene
- **c** obtuse
- **d** isosceles

6 What fraction is coloured?

a $\frac{1}{4}$ **b** $\frac{1}{6}$

c $\frac{1}{3}$ **d** $\frac{1}{5}$

7 What is the time?

a 6.55 **b** 6.07

c 6.53 **d** 7.53

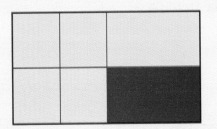

8 Which sign is missing?

a = **b** <

c > **d** ≈

9 ☐ 54

9 What is the reading?

a $4\frac{1}{2}$ kg **b** 4.25 kg

c 5 kg **d** 4.1 kg

10 How many degrees?

a 90° **b** 45°

c 180° **d** 135°

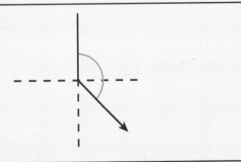

Check your answers on page 96. ✓

Place value

100 000	200 000	300 000	400 000	500 000	600 000	700 000	800 000	900 000
10 000	20 000	30 000	40 000	50 000	60 000	70 000	80 000	90 000
1000	2000	3000	4000	5000	6000	7000	8000	9000
100	200	300	400	500	600	700	800	900
10	20	30	40	50	60	70	80	90
1	2	3	4	5	6	7	8	9

Starters

Write in figures.

1 sixty-eight thousand
2 fifty thousand and twenty
3 ninety-nine thousand and nine
4 six thousand and sixty
5 four hundred thousand

Write in words.

6 65 040
7 80 750
8 52 500
9 700 000
10 1 000 000

Practice

A Write the value of the red digit.

1 36 471	2 50 377

3 64 732

4 120 377   5 704 266   6 124 326

7 1 350 000   8 2 750 000   9 4 180 000

B Write these numbers in figures.

1 fifteen thousand   2 nine thousand and four   3 thirty-two thousand

4 half a million   5 four hundred thousand   6 six-and-a-half million

C Copy and complete the tables.

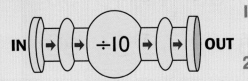

IN → → ÷10 → → OUT

1
IN	4250	3150	7500	6000
OUT				

2
IN				
OUT	59	401	730	900

D Copy and complete the tables.

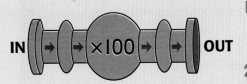

IN → → ×100 → → OUT

1
IN	530	708	518	9200
OUT				

2
IN				
OUT	5100	87 000	30 700	950 000

Challenge

Draw a line to show 0 to 1000.

0   1000

Mark the approximate positions of these numbers.

 980   675   154   418

Number patterns

1	2	3	4	5	6	7	8	9	10
2	4	6	8	10	12	14	16	18	20
3	6	9	12	15	18	21	24	27	30
4	8	12	16	20	24	28	32	36	40
5	10	15	20	25	30	35	40	45	50
6	12	18	24	30	36	42	48	54	60
7	14	21	28	35	42	49	56	63	70
8	16	24	32	40	48	56	64	72	80
9	18	27	36	45	54	63	72	81	90
10	20	30	40	50	60	70	80	90	100

Starters

Look at the blue square.

1 Multiply the numbers which are diagonally opposite. What do you notice?

Try squares of your own. Does this always happen?

Look at the yellow cross.

2 Total the four outer numbers. Divide the middle number into the total.

Try this with other crosses like the yellow one. Write down what you notice.

Practice

A Write the answers to these.

1 $7 \times 8 =$ 　　　2 $9 \times 9 =$ 　　　3 $6 \times 4 =$ 　　　4 $7 \times 7 =$

5 $36 \div 9 =$ 　　　6 $42 \div 7 =$ 　　　7 $45 \div 9 =$ 　　　8 $54 \div 6 =$

9 $40 \times 50 =$ 　　10 $30 \times 70 =$ 　　11 $50 \times 50 =$ 　　12 $70 \times 20 =$

13 $600 \div 10 =$ 　　14 $320 \div 10 =$ 　　15 $560 \div 10 =$ 　　16 $700 \div 10 =$

B Work these out.

Always work out what is in the brackets first.

1 $(3 \times 4) + 20 =$ 　　　2 $(7 \times 9) - 40 =$ 　　　3 $(6 \times 6) + 64 =$

4 $(9 \times 8) - 62 =$ 　　　5 $(7 \times 4) + 99 =$ 　　　6 $(3 \times 6) + (5 \times 8) =$

7 $(4 \times 4) + (9 \times 9) =$ 　　8 $(8 \times 6) - (8 \times 4) =$ 　　9 $(5 \times 8) - (6 \times 4) =$

C Try these.

1 It is eight weeks to the School Fair.
How many days is this?

2 Raffle tickets come in books of 500.
How many tickets will be in 6 books?

3 It will cost 25p to enter the raffle.
How many people will be needed to make £75?

4 A treasure hunt board game has 144 small squares.
The board is 9 squares wide. How long is it?

Remember

Always work out what is in the brackets first.

Challenge

Use the digits 1, 2, 3, 4, brackets and +, −, × and ÷.

Investigate sums which have answers in the range 1 to 12.

You must use each digit once and once only in each sum.

For example, $(4 \times 3) - (1 \times 2) = 10$.

Try to find an example of each answer 1 to 12.

Try to find different solutions for the answer 10.

Multiplication

Use digit cards.

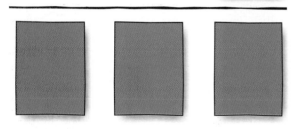

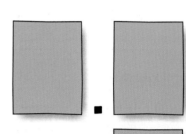

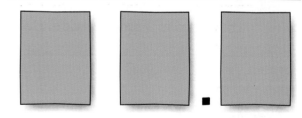

Starters

1   Write 10 different multiplications for the red sum.

2   Write a rule for not getting four digits in the answer.

3   Write 10 different multiplications for the green sum.

4   Write a rule for getting two digits before the decimal point.

Practice

A **1** **Double each number.**

46	32	85	39	66	54	37	99

2 **Halve each number.**

24	36	52	70	46	58	92	86

B Try these.

1	342 × 5	2	433 × 4	3	596 × 3	4	408 × 7	5	663 × 6	6	496 × 8

7	698 × 9	8	756 × 7	9	568 × 5	10	468 × 6	11	545 × 9	12	679 × 3

C Try these.

1	5.4 × 3	2	6.7 × 4	3	2.9 × 2	4	7.6 × 5	5	6.8 × 8	6	9.1 × 9

7	2.4 × 9	8	3.8 × 6	9	4.9 × 9	10	7.6 × 8	11	4.3 × 7	12	8.8 × 8

Challenge

On a calculator you can only touch  Find a way to answer these. 272 × 5

256 × 3

Fractions

$\frac{1}{2}$	$\frac{1}{3}$	$\frac{2}{3}$	$\frac{1}{4}$	$\frac{2}{4}$	$\frac{3}{4}$
$\frac{1}{5}$	$\frac{2}{5}$	$\frac{3}{5}$	$\frac{4}{5}$	$\frac{1}{6}$	$\frac{2}{6}$
$\frac{3}{6}$	$\frac{4}{6}$	$\frac{5}{6}$	$\frac{1}{8}$	$\frac{2}{8}$	$\frac{3}{8}$
$\frac{4}{8}$	$\frac{5}{8}$	$\frac{6}{8}$	$\frac{7}{8}$	$\frac{1}{10}$	$\frac{2}{10}$
$\frac{3}{10}$	$\frac{4}{10}$	$\frac{5}{10}$	$\frac{6}{10}$	$\frac{7}{10}$	$\frac{8}{10}$
$\frac{9}{10}$	$\frac{1}{12}$	$\frac{2}{12}$	$\frac{3}{12}$	$\frac{4}{12}$	$\frac{5}{12}$
$\frac{6}{12}$	$\frac{7}{12}$	$\frac{8}{12}$	$\frac{9}{12}$	$\frac{10}{12}$	$\frac{11}{12}$

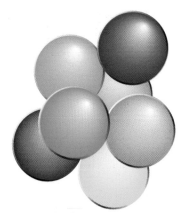

Starters

Look at the grid.

1. Write 3 fractions equivalent to $\frac{1}{2}$.

2. Write 2 fractions equivalent to $\frac{3}{4}$.

3. Write 3 fractions which are more than $\frac{1}{2}$.

4. Write 3 fractions which are less than $\frac{1}{4}$.

5. Write 3 tenths fractions which cannot be cancelled.

Practice

A Change each fraction to a mixed number.

1 $\frac{11}{2}$ 2 $\frac{13}{3}$ 3 $\frac{37}{10}$ 4 $\frac{17}{4}$ 5 $\frac{25}{8}$ 6 $\frac{61}{10}$

7 $\frac{33}{2}$ 8 $\frac{23}{3}$ 9 $\frac{19}{8}$ 10 $\frac{31}{8}$ 11 $\frac{59}{10}$ 12 $\frac{39}{4}$

B Change each mixed number to an improper fraction.

1 $1\frac{3}{4}$ 2 $2\frac{7}{8}$ 3 $2\frac{3}{10}$ 4 $9\frac{2}{3}$ 5 $3\frac{5}{8}$ 6 $4\frac{1}{2}$

7 $5\frac{2}{3}$ 8 $8\frac{1}{3}$ 9 $6\frac{3}{4}$ 10 $8\frac{1}{10}$ 11 $7\frac{2}{3}$ 12 $9\frac{4}{5}$

C Copy and complete these equivalent fractions.

1

$$\frac{8}{10} = \frac{\square}{5}$$

2

$$\frac{6}{8} = \frac{3}{\square}$$

3

$$\frac{8}{\square} = \frac{4}{\square}$$

4

$$\frac{4}{\square} = \frac{\square}{3}$$

5

$$\frac{\square}{16} = \frac{\square}{8}$$

6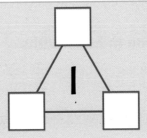

$$\frac{6}{\square} = \frac{\square}{3}$$

Challenge

The corner numbers total 1.

Find three solutions.

Hundredths

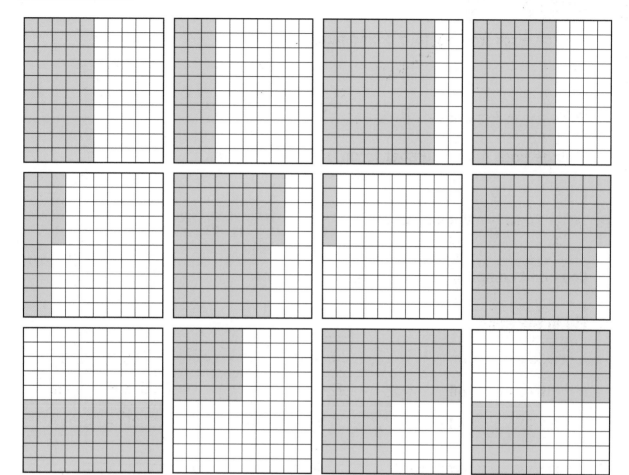

Cancel each fraction.

1 $\frac{50}{100}$	**2** $\frac{10}{100}$	**3** $\frac{30}{100}$	**4** $\frac{80}{100}$	**5** $\frac{90}{100}$
6 $\frac{25}{100}$	**7** $\frac{75}{100}$	**8** $\frac{5}{100}$	**9** $\frac{15}{100}$	**10** $\frac{55}{100}$

Write each fraction in hundredths.

1 $\frac{1}{10}$	**2** $\frac{6}{10}$	**3** $\frac{9}{10}$	**4** $\frac{7}{10}$	**5** $\frac{3}{10}$
6 $\frac{1}{2}$	**7** $\frac{1}{5}$	**8** $\frac{1}{4}$	**9** $\frac{3}{4}$	**10** $\frac{4}{5}$

Practice

0   0.5   1

A Write these fractions as decimals.

1 $\frac{3}{10}$ 2 $\frac{7}{10}$ 3 $\frac{8}{10}$ 4 $4\frac{5}{10}$ 5 $3\frac{9}{10}$ 6 $7\frac{4}{10}$

7 $5\frac{2}{10}$ 8 $9\frac{3}{10}$ 9 $6\frac{1}{10}$ 10 $7\frac{6}{10}$ 11 $4\frac{1}{2}$ 12 $5\frac{1}{2}$

B Write these fractions as decimals.

1 $\frac{30}{100}$ 2 $\frac{70}{100}$ 3 $\frac{50}{100}$ 4 $\frac{80}{100}$ 5 $\frac{90}{100}$ 6 $\frac{20}{100}$

7 $\frac{25}{100}$ 8 $\frac{75}{100}$ 9 $\frac{15}{100}$ 10 $\frac{6}{100}$ 11 $\frac{4}{100}$ 12 $\frac{1}{100}$

C Fill in the gaps.

1   2.5 km = ☐ m   2   1.5 m = ☐ cm   3   4.5 kg = ☐ g

4   3.5 l = ☐ ml   5   £2.45 = ☐ p   6   3.75 m = ☐ cm

7   2.25 l = ☐ ml   8   3.75 kg = ☐ g   9   £7.05 = ☐ p

D Write these percentages as a fraction.

1   10%   2   50%   3   90%

4   25%   5   75%   6   20%

7   17%   8   5%   9   1%

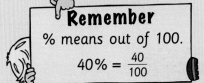

Remember

% means out of 100.

$40\% = \frac{40}{100}$

Challenge

How many red cubes are there for each white cube?

Investigate different-sized rectangles which have the same ratio as this.

15

Handling data

Use the graph.

1 Why do you think the measures are approximate?

2 How deep is the deepest sea?

3 Which sea is approximately 250 metres deep?

4 What is the difference in depth between the English Channel and the Red Sea?

5 Which two seas have a difference in depth of about 500 metres?

6 Which seas are over a kilometre deep?

Practice

A This chart shows 100 rolls on a dice.

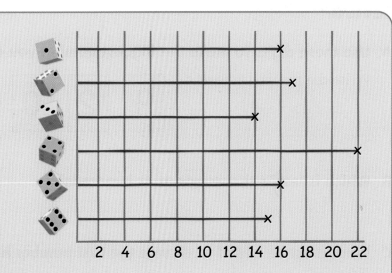

1 Which number was rolled most often?

2 Which numbers were rolled 16 times?

3 Which frequency is the mode?

4 What is the range of frequencies?

B Talk about these chances.

no chance   even chance   certain

 rolling a six

someone telephoning you tonight

turning over a black card

thick snow tomorrow

 spinning two coins to get two heads

having a birthday today

Challenge

Roll 2 dice.

Find the total.

Investigate which totals are most likely to occur.

Review

A Use these digits to make the biggest number you can.

Write the number in words.

| 9 | 2 | 0 | 5 | 0 | 6 | 3 |

B Which is less, 6 thousands or 61 hundreds?

C What must be added to change the first number into the second?

| 32 546 | 82 546 |

D Multiply each number by 100.

1 47   **2** 800   **3** 5000   **4** 10 000

E Talk about numbers which are between

5 and 5.5

F Which numbers are missing from the tables?

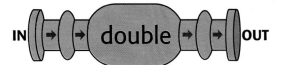

1

IN	28	39	57	66
OUT				

2

IN				
OUT	48	54	78	90

G **What is the approximate answer?**

Work out the exact answer.

$$586 \times 6$$

H **What is the approximate answer?**

Work out the exact answer.

$$5.8 \times 6$$

I **Which is the odd one out in each set?**

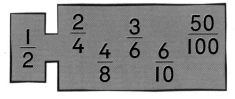

1 $\frac{1}{2}$ $\quad$ $\frac{2}{4}$ $\quad$ $\frac{3}{6}$ $\quad$ $\frac{50}{100}$ $\quad$ $\frac{4}{8}$ $\quad$ $\frac{6}{10}$

2 $\frac{3}{4}$ $\quad$ $\frac{9}{16}$ $\quad$ $\frac{8}{12}$ $\quad$ $\frac{6}{8}$ $\quad$ $\frac{15}{20}$ $\quad$ $\frac{75}{100}$

J **What is the digit 4 worth in each of these numbers?**

$$34625 \qquad 5.45 \qquad 7.34$$

K **Which of these is not the same as $\frac{1}{2}$?**

$$50\% \qquad 0.5 \qquad \frac{50}{100} \qquad \frac{5}{10} \qquad \frac{5}{100}$$

L **Answer these.**

1 Make this into a mixed number. $\quad$ $\frac{21}{4}$

2 Make this into an improper fraction. $\quad$ $4\frac{7}{8}$

19

Shapes

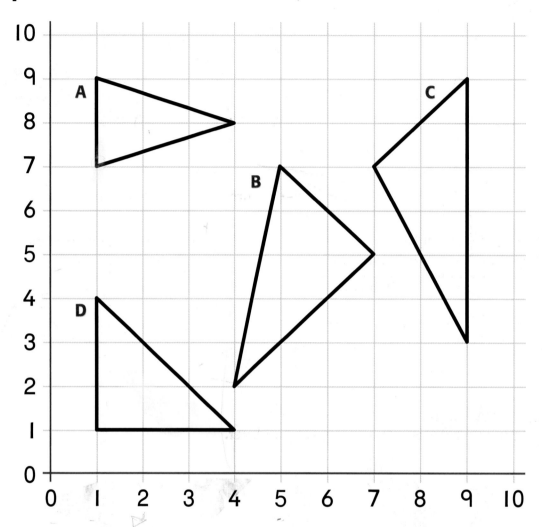

Starters

1 Which triangles are isosceles?

2 Which triangles are scalene?

3 Which triangles are right-angled?

4 Which triangle is right-angled and isosceles?

5 Which triangle has the co-ordinates (4, 2), (7, 5), (5, 7)?

6 Write the co-ordinate of a point inside triangle D.

7 Write the co-ordinate of a point on the side of triangle A.

8 Write the co-ordinates of the vertices of triangle C.

Practice

A True or false?

1 Rectangles have parallel sides.

2 A square is a special rectangle.

3 The diagonals of a rectangle are lines of symmetry.

4 Opposite sides of a rectangle are equal.

5 The four internal angles of a rectangle add up to 360°.

6 If you cut the corner off a rectangle you are left with a hexagon.

B Look at the triangles.
Copy and complete the table.

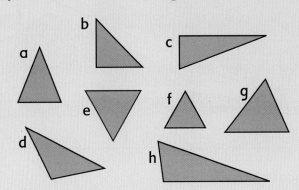

name	triangle
equilateral	
isosceles	
scalene	

C Copy each shape.
Draw what each one looks like flipped over.

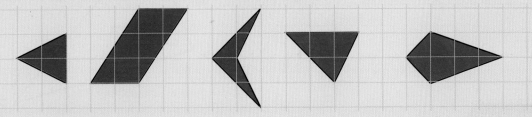

Challenge

Pentominoes are made from 5 squares.

How many can you find?

Which have a line of symmetry?

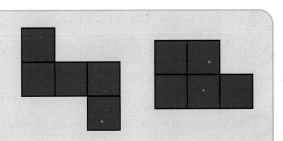

Measuring and perimeters

scale

1 cm on the plan = 300 cm in the garden

0   1500 m

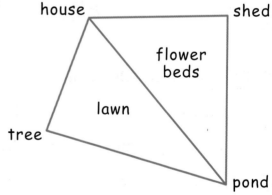

Starters

1   Will the distances on the plan be exact or approximate?

2   What is the distance from the house to the pond?

3   How far is it from the tree to the shed by the shortest path?

4   What is the perimeter of the flower beds?

5   What is the perimeter of the lawn?

6   What is the perimeter of the whole garden?

Practice

A Here are the results of a flea hopping competition.

Start

Boris

Eric

Mollie

Freda

Henry

Norman

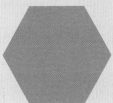

To the nearest mm, how far did each flea jump?

B Measure the sides of these shapes to the nearest mm.
Calculate the perimeter of each regular shape.

   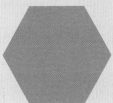

C Copy and complete these.

1 1 km = ☐ m

2 1 m = ☐ cm

3 1 m = ☐ mm

4 1 cm = ☐ mm

5 $\frac{1}{2}$ km = ☐ m

6 $\frac{1}{4}$ m = ☐ cm

7 $\frac{3}{4}$ m = ☐ cm

8 $\frac{1}{2}$ cm = ☐ mm

9 500 mm = ☐ cm

10 3000 m = ☐ km

11 800 cm = ☐ m

12 4000 mm = ☐ m

Challenge

Draw shapes which have perimeters of 24 cm.

Investigate how the area changes.

23

Measuring problems

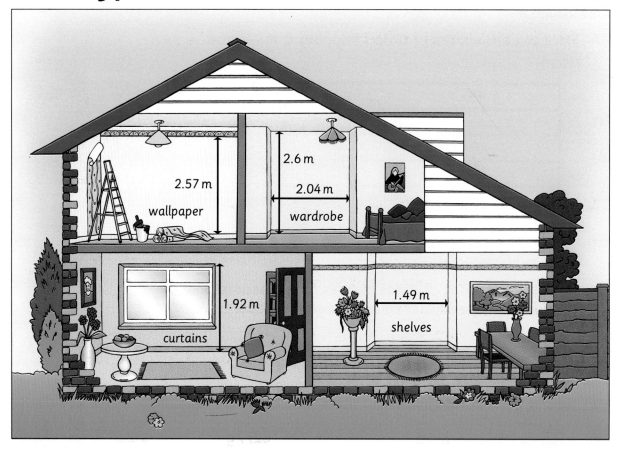

Labels on diagram:
- 2.57 m — wallpaper
- 2.6 m
- 2.04 m — wardrobe
- 1.92 m — curtains
- 1.49 m — shelves

Starters

1 Two floor-length curtains are needed. What is the total length?

2 How much will be left from a 5.7 m roll of curtain material?

3 Shelves are sold in 3.7 m lengths. How many lengths are needed for 5 shelves?

4 What length will be wasted when each shelf is cut?

5 Wallpaper is in 10-metre rolls. How many lengths can be cut from one roll?

6 Eight rolls of paper are needed which cost £7.99 a roll.
What will be the change from four £20 notes?

7 The wardrobe is 1.75 m tall. How much space would be above it?

8 Fit a wardrobe that is 1.26 m wide in the middle of the alcove.
How much space will be each side?

Practice

A How long have these cakes been in the oven?

1	In	11.55		2	In	13.10		3	In	15.40
	Out	12.35			Out	14.05			Out	16.25

4	In	16.54		5	In	15.03		6	In	19.10
	Out	17.28			Out	15.51			Out	20.01

B Here is a drawing of part of a long tape measure.

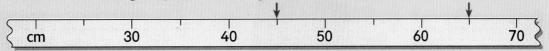

1 What is the distance between the arrows?
2 How many millimetres is it from one arrow to the next?
3 How many metres is it from the start of the tape to the first arrow?
4 How many metres is it from the start of the tape to the second arrow?

C Round each measurement to the nearest whole unit.

1 3175 ml ≈ ☐ litres   2 8277 g ≈ ☐ kilograms

3 7951 mm ≈ ☐ metres   4 5.7 kg ≈ ☐ kg

5 3.45 l ≈ ☐ l   6 7.45 m ≈ ☐ m

Challenge

Make two of these from thin card.

Fasten them together
at the edges.

Try to fold the
model to make
a tetrahedron.

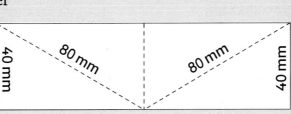

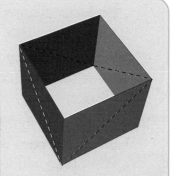

Calculations

Starters

1 How many days are there in six weeks?

2 How many weeks are there in six months?

3 How many of the egg boxes are needed for 46 eggs?

4 Eggs cost £1.30 a dozen. How much would $2\frac{1}{2}$ dozen cost?

5 How many cola cans would be in 14 packs?

6 A six-pack costs £1.49. What would 5 packs cost?

7 Pru saves £3 each month. How long before she saves £34?

8 Andy saves £8 each month. How much more has Andy than Pru after 7 months?

9 Fence panels are 6 feet long. How many will be needed for 48 feet?

10 Panels cost £10.25 each. How much will the 48-feet long fence cost?

11 A cake goes in the oven at 11.53 for 35 minutes. What time will it come out?

12 The cake must cool for 45 minutes. When can it be eaten?

Practice

A What is the difference between these pairs?

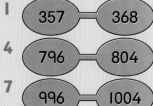

1 357 — 368

2 1634 — 1647

3 3017 — 3024

4 796 — 804

5 2495 — 2506

6 6198 — 6207

7 996 — 1004

8 3994 — 4006

9 7991 — 8012

B Try these.

1 456 + 978	2 647 + 895	3 776 + 758	4 587 + 685
5 3784 + 965	6 3684 + 965	7 7256 + 849	8 5805 + 698

C Try these.

1 843 − 698	2 504 − 178	3 680 − 382	4 813 − 648
5 1365 − 728	6 5040 − 392	7 6140 − 785	8 8106 − 816

Challenge

Forbidden key

Use a calculator to answer these, but …

You are not allowed to touch the **7** key.

Explore different ways of doing this.

5737
+ 478

3702
+ 874

Number patterns

18	63	16	33	50	31	48	1
35	14	19	62	3	46	51	30
64	17	34	15	32	49	2	47
13	36	61	20	45	4	29	52
60	21	40	9	56	25	44	5
37	12	57	24	41	8	53	28
22	59	10	39	26	55	6	43
11	38	23	58	7	42	27	54

**A Swiss mathematician called Leonard Euler designed
this special number square in the 18th century.**

Starters

1 Write something you notice about the square.
2 What do you notice about the row totals?
3 What do you notice about the column totals?
4 What do you notice about the diagonal totals?
5 What do you notice about the totals in the coloured blocks?

Practice

A Copy and complete each sequence.

1	156	165	174	183	___	___	___ ___
2	330	370	410	450	___	___	___ ___
3	852	822	792	762	___	___	___ ___
4	11	8	5	2	___	___	___ ___
5	84	54	24	−14	___	___	___

B What are these?

1 4^2 2 7^2 3 5^2 4 9^2 5 10^2

6 2^2 7 1^2 8 6^2 9 8^2 10 20^2

> **Remember**
>
> A short way of writing 3×3 is 3^2. $3^2 = 9$.

C List all the factors you know for these numbers.

1 25   2 36   3 42   4 72   5 80   6 99

D Write all the numbers you know, up to 30, which have only one pair of factors.

Challenge

Investigate what happens if you total:

- pairs of consecutive odd numbers,
- three consecutive odd numbers,
- four consecutive odd numbers.

Review

A Name each type of triangle.

1    2   3   4

B Which shapes are at these co-ordinates?

1   (3, 2)

2   (4, 3)

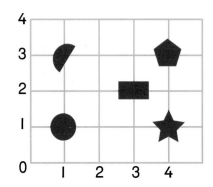

C Which of these shapes have lines of symmetry?

1   2   3   4

D Calculate the perimeter of these shapes.

1   45 mm   2   3

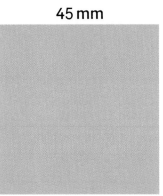

45 mm

16 mm

28 mm

12 mm

24 mm

12 mm

12 mm

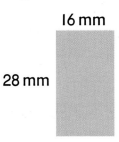

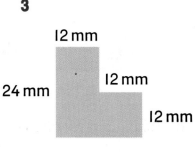

E Measure each line to the nearest mm.

1

2

3

F What are the missing measurements?

1 3.75 m = ☐ cm   2 5.5 kg = ☐ g   3 7.25 l = ☐ ml

G What is the difference in time between 13:48 and 14:16?

H Answer these.

1 $\begin{array}{r} 578 \\ + 694 \\ \hline \end{array}$ 2 $\begin{array}{r} 3840 \\ + 684 \\ \hline \end{array}$

I Answer these.

1 $\begin{array}{r} 705 \\ - 58 \\ \hline \end{array}$ 2 $\begin{array}{r} 3040 \\ - 787 \\ \hline \end{array}$

J What is the square of these?

1 6   2 9   3 7   4 10

K Which number between 25 and 30 has only one pair of factors?

L This is part of a counting pattern.

11 ____ ____   −4

What could the missing numbers be?

31

Do you remember?

1   What is this number?

100 000

   a   one million   **b**   ten thousand

   c   hundred thousand   **d**   ten million

2   What is $\frac{1}{10}$ of 560?

   a   5600   **b**   56   **c**   5.6   **d**   0.56

3   Multiplying by 25 is the same as:

   a   multiplying by 100 then dividing by 4

   b   multiplying by 100 then halving

   c   multiplying by 100 then subtracting 25

   d   multiplying by 100 then subtracting 50

4   Two thirds is the same as:

   a $\frac{4}{9}$ **b** $\frac{6}{12}$ **c** $\frac{3}{10}$ **d** $\frac{4}{6}$

5 $\frac{40}{100}$ is the same as:

   a   4.00   **b**   0.04   **c**   0.40   **d**   4.40

6 **How many lines of symmetry has this rectangle?**

a 1 **b** 2 **c** 3 **d** 4

7 **What is the name of this triangle?**

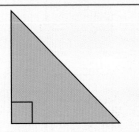

a isosceles **b** equilateral **c** scalene

8 **How many millimetres are there in 1.5 metres?**

a 150 **b** 1500 **c** 15 000 **d** 15

9 **Which time is the same as 4.55 p.m.?**

a 04.55 **b** 05.55 **c** 16.55 **d** 17.05

10 **How many millimetres is this reading?**

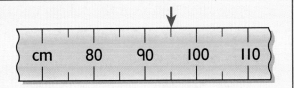

a 90 **b** 95 **c** 950 **d** 9500

Check your answers on page 96. ✓

Place value

Use digit cards.

Starters

Use one set of digit cards.

1 Place digit cards on the red markers.

 Each number should be about 50.

 Which number sentences can you make?

2 Place digit cards on the yellow markers.

 Each number should be about 75.

 Which number sentences can you make?

3 Place digit cards on the blue markers.

 Each number should be about 40.

 Which number sentences can you make?

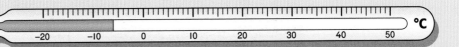

Practice

A

1 The thermometer rises by 15 °C. What is the new temperature?

2 The temperature falls from 88 °C to –3 °C. What is the drop in temperature?

3 The temperature is 3 °C and falls by 12 °C. What is the new temperature?

4 The temperature is –12 °C. How much must it rise to reach 6 °C?

5 What is the difference in temperature between –13 °C and 17 °C?

B Estimate the position of each arrow.

1 −5 ↓ 0   2 −10 ↓ 0

3 −20 ↓ 0   4 −5 ↓ 5

C Which numbers could go in the boxes?

1 $-10 < \boxed{} < 0$ 2 $-10 > \boxed{} > -15$ 3 $-5 \le \boxed{} \le 0$

4 $24 \le \boxed{} \le 30$ 5 $500 \ge \boxed{} \ge 450$ 6 $1000 \le \boxed{} \le 2000$

D Write these numbers in order with the smallest first.

1 –10 °C, 12 °C, –20 °C, 4 °C   2 –45, –75, 45, 75

3 350 mm, 305 m, 350 m, 305 cm   4 45 g, 45 kg, 54 g, 54 kg

5 3500 ml, 5300 ml, 3050 ml, 5030 ml   6 460 km, 6400 m, 640 km, 460 m

Challenge

You must touch these keys at least once.

Any symbol key can be used.

No other number keys can be used.

How can you reach –5?

Multiplication and division

100								
90								
80	81							
70	72							
60	63	64						
50	54	56						
40	42	45	48	49				
30	32	35	36					
20	21	24	25	27	28			
10	12	14	15	16	18			
1	2	3	4	5	6	7	8	9

You will find all these numbers in a multiplication grid.

List of factors for 24 → 1, 2, 3, 4, 6, 8, 12, 24

Factor pairs for 24 → (1, 24), (2, 12), (3, 8), (4, 6)

Starters

Write lists of factors for these.

1 28 **2** 32 **3** 42

4 64 **5** 90

Write factor pairs for these.

6 36 **7** 48 **8** 56

9 72 **10** 100

Practice

A Answer these.

Remember: work out brackets first.

1 (5 × 7) + 40 =   2 (80 × 2) − 50 =   3 100 − (20 × 3) =

4 100 − (50 ÷ 2) =   5 (3 × 8) + (7 × 8) =   6 (56 ÷ 7) × (63 ÷ 9) =

7 (9 × 4) ÷ (24 ÷ 6) =   8 (8 × 8) − (3 × 12) =   9 (30 × 5) − 20 =

B Find out where to put brackets in these problems.

1 8 + 6 × 2 = 28   2 20 + 12 ÷ 3 = 24

3 19 − 3 × 5 = 4   4 13 − 1 ÷ 4 = 3

5 10 + 2 × 6 − 4 = 18   6 36 − 16 ÷ 4 + 8 = 40

7 9 × 8 + 4 × 7 = 100   8 18 + 3 − 7 ÷ 7 = 2

Remember

Always work out what is in the brackets first.

C Try these.

1 30 × 50 =   2 36 × 20 =   3 80 × 70 =
   29 × 50 =   36 × 19 =   80 × 69 =

4 3600 ÷ 100 =   5 8724 ÷ 2 =   6 1470 ÷ 7 =
   3600 ÷ 25 =   8724 ÷ 4 =   1470 ÷ 14 =

D What could the missing number be?

1 15 × 6 = 15 × ☐ × 2   2 75 × 8 = 75 × 4 × ☐

3 75 × 24 = 25 × ☐ × ☐ × 6   4 36 × 25 = 4 × ☐ × 5 × ☐

5 90 ÷ 6 = 90 ÷ ☐ ÷ 2   6 720 ÷ 8 = 720 ÷ 2 ÷ ☐

7 360 ÷ 6 = 360 ÷ ☐ ÷ ☐   8 420 ÷ 15 = 420 ÷ ☐ ÷ ☐

Challenge

Use each of these digits once and once only.

Use the signs + , −, × and ÷.

Make an answer of ☐1☐ .

example (3 + 2) − (4 × 1)

Problems

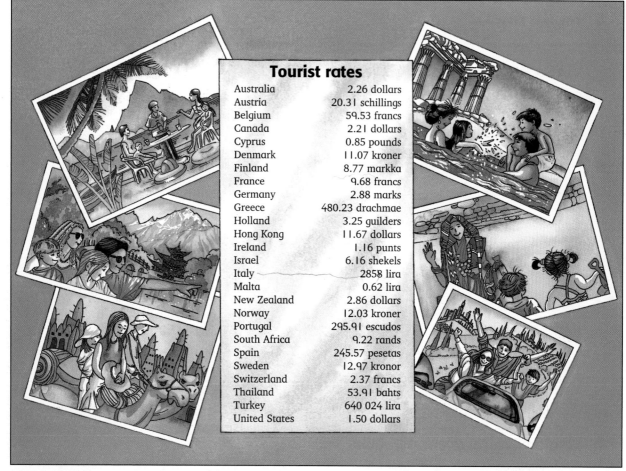

Tourist rates

Australia	2.26 dollars
Austria	20.31 schillings
Belgium	59.53 francs
Canada	2.21 dollars
Cyprus	0.85 pounds
Denmark	11.07 kroner
Finland	8.77 markka
France	9.68 francs
Germany	2.88 marks
Greece	480.23 drachmae
Holland	3.25 guilders
Hong Kong	11.67 dollars
Ireland	1.16 punts
Israel	6.16 shekels
Italy	2858 lira
Malta	0.62 lira
New Zealand	2.86 dollars
Norway	12.03 kroner
Portugal	295.91 escudos
South Africa	9.22 rands
Spain	245.57 pesetas
Sweden	12.97 kronor
Switzerland	2.37 francs
Thailand	53.91 bahts
Turkey	640 024 lira
United States	1.50 dollars

This table shows how much foreign money £1 will buy.

Starters

1 How many Maltese lira will £50 buy?

2 How many German marks will £100 buy?

3 Approximately how much would 2000 French francs cost in pounds?

4 Approximately how much would 1 million Italian lira cost in pounds?

5 Choose a country for a holiday.

Make a simple ready reckoner to help you with the money.

Practice

A Work these out in your head.

1 $30 \times 400 =$ 2 $800 \times 40 =$ 3 $145 \times 2 =$ 4 $340 \times \frac{1}{2} =$

5 $600 \times 9 =$ 6 $6 \times 70 =$ 7 $24 \times 3 =$ 8 $4 \times 18 =$

9 $\frac{1}{2} \times 64 =$ 10 $50 \times 60 =$ 11 $60 \times 700 =$ 12 $250 \times 2 =$

B Calculate these.

1	2	3	4	5
346	577	608	764	477
× 4	× 7	× 9	× 8	× 5

6	7	8	9	10
818	645	368	546	727
× 8	× 7	× 4	× 3	× 9

C Answer these.

1 One tin weighs 173 g.
   What would 6 tins weigh?

2 Tickets are £7.25 each.
   What would 8 tickets cost?

3 I have three 5 ml spoons of medicine
   each day.
   How much medicine do I have in
   2 weeks?

4 Fence panels are 1.24 m long.
   How far would 7 panels stretch?

5 I have £185 but my sister has
   double this. How much have
   we altogether?

6 How much is four 205 ml tins
   and five 197 ml tins altogether?

Challenge

$$
\begin{array}{r} 39 \\ \times\ 62 \\ \hline 2418 \end{array}
$$

Switch the digits around. ➡

$$
\begin{array}{r} 93 \\ \times\ 26 \\ \hline 2418 \end{array}
$$

Try to find another pair which does this.

Division and problems

Fares

single fares

Cars — £12
Vans — £15
Coaches — £24
Lorries — £32
Cycles — £4
Passengers — £6

The table shows vehicles and passengers carried on one return journey.

	Outward	Return
Cars	26	36
Vans	13	10
Coaches	8	12
Lorries	11	8
Cycles	0	2
Passengers	625	680

Starters

1 How many passengers were carried during the day?

2 How many vehicles were carried during the day?

3 What was the income from the vans for the day?

4 What was the income from the passengers for the day?

5 What was the income from the cars for the day?

6 How much was earned by the ferry that day?

Practice

A Work these out in your head.

1 8200 ÷ 100 =   2 7600 ÷ 100 =   3 9100 ÷ 100 =   4 6600 ÷ 100 =

5 5400 ÷ 10 =   6 6300 ÷ 10 =   7 9900 ÷ 10 =   8 9400 ÷ 10 =

9 ☐ ÷ 100 = 34   10 ☐ ÷ 100 = 50   11 ☐ ÷ 10 = 740

12 ☐ ÷ 10 = 76   13 4600 ÷ ☐ = 46   14 9300 ÷ ☐ = 930

B Calculate these.

1 436 ÷ 5 =   2 742 ÷ 6 =   3 364 ÷ 4 =   4 816 ÷ 7 =

5 634 ÷ 3 =   6 556 ÷ 9 =   7 621 ÷ 8 =   8 382 ÷ 3 =

9 569 ÷ 4 =   10 777 ÷ 8 =   11 610 ÷ 9 =   12 584 ÷ 8 =

C What is the missing number?

1 ☐ ÷ 4 = 56 r3   2 ☐ ÷ 6 = 27 r4   3 ☐ ÷ 9 = 17 r6

4 ☐ ÷ 5 = 42 r4   5 ☐ ÷ 3 = 44 r1   6 ☐ ÷ 7 = 36 r5

D Which digits are hidden?

1 4) 2●4   (56)

2 6) 4●●   (78)

3 5) 42●   (●5)

4 ●) 792   (99)

5 4) ●●4●   (236)

6 7) 8●6   (11●)

7 3) 83●   (27●)

8 ●) 888   (14●)

Challenge

Use digit cards 0 to 9.

Use any operation cards.

Find ways of reaching 7.

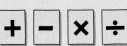

41

Fractions and decimals

Starters

Round each number to the nearest whole number.

1	4.3	**2**	2.5	**3**	6.2	**4**	0.7	**5**	5.8
6	1.74	**7**	2.56	**8**	6.09	**9**	5.36	**10**	8.91

Write each set in order.
Start with the smallest.

11 2.04   2.41   2.14   2.40   **12** 5.73   5.37   3.57   3.75

13 8.64   6.84   8.46   4.68   **14** 6.17   7.16   6.71   7.61

15 9.29   9.92   2.99   9.90

Practice

A Place these in order, starting with the smallest.

1 $1\frac{1}{2}$ $\frac{1}{2}$ 2 $\frac{1}{4}$ $1\frac{3}{4}$ 2 $\frac{3}{4}$ $1\frac{1}{3}$ $\frac{1}{2}$ $1\frac{1}{2}$

3 $\frac{7}{10}$ $\frac{1}{2}$ $1\frac{1}{4}$ $1\frac{1}{2}$ 4 $2\frac{1}{4}$ $1\frac{3}{4}$ $2\frac{1}{3}$ $1\frac{1}{3}$

5 $1\frac{1}{3}$ $\frac{3}{10}$ $\frac{3}{4}$ $1\frac{3}{4}$ 6 $\frac{2}{5}$ $\frac{7}{10}$ $1\frac{1}{3}$ $1\frac{1}{10}$

B What fraction of a metre are the following?

1 50 cm   2 25 cm   3 75 cm   4 10 cm   5 20 cm

What fraction of £1 are the following?

6 25p   7 75p   8 5p   9 10p   10 90p

C What is $\frac{1}{10}$ of these?

1 60   2 70   3 600   4 340   5 730   6 610

What is $\frac{1}{100}$ of these?

7 400   8 4000   9 9000   10 800   11 3000   12 600

D Try these.

1 Write $\frac{3}{4}$ of £1 in pence.   2 Write $\frac{7}{10}$ of 1 metre in centimetres.

3 Write $\frac{2}{3}$ of 1 hour in minutes.   4 Write $\frac{3}{10}$ of 1 kilogram in grams.

5 Write $\frac{23}{100}$ of £1 in pence.   6 Write $\frac{57}{100}$ of 1 metre in centimetres.

7 Write $\frac{41}{100}$ of 1 kilogram in grams.   8 Write $\frac{7}{100}$ of 1 litre in millilitres.

Challenge

Investigate fractions on a calculator.

Which fractions do not make recurring decimals?

Which fractions do make recurring decimals?

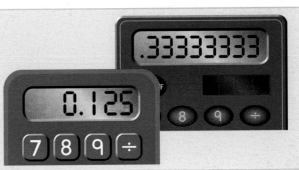

43

Shapes

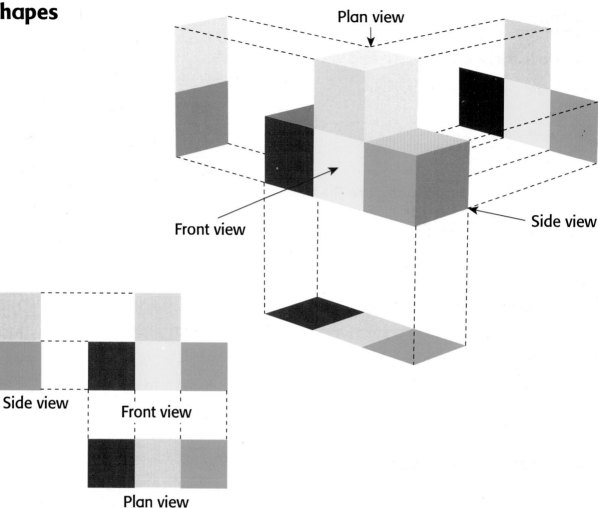

Starters

Use cubes to build these two models.

Side view

Front view

Plan view

Practice

A Look at the shapes.

Write their letters in the table.

Has parallel sides	
Has right angles	
Has acute angles	
Has obtuse angles	

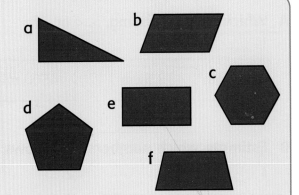

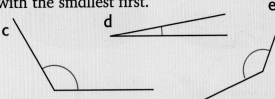

B Look at these angles.

1 Say whether each angle is acute or obtuse.

2 Estimate the size of each angle.

3 Measure the size of each angle.

4 Write the angles in order of size, with the smallest first.

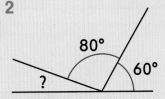

C Calculate the missing angles.

1

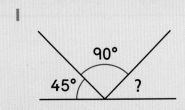

90°
45°   ?

2

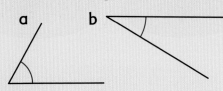

80°
?   60°

3

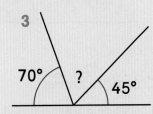

70°   ?
45°

Challenge

This tile made this rotation pattern.

Design your own tile.

Make a rotation pattern.

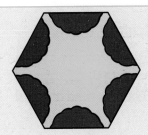

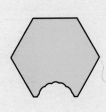

45

Review

A Which sign is missing, >, < or =?

1
35 mm ☐ 3.5 cm

2
4500 ml ☐ 4 litres

3
2.5 kg ☐ 2600 g

B Estimate which numbers the arrows are pointing to.

1
–10 ────────────── 0

2
0 ────────────── 100

3
0 ────────────── 1000

C Put these in order starting with the smallest.

64 500   465 000   6500   654 000

D Calculate these.

1 (40 × 3) − (60 ÷ 2)

2 (30 × 40) ÷ (100 − 60)

E Calculate these.

1 574 × 6

2 387 × 8

F Calculate these.

1 495 ÷ 4

2 788 ÷ 6

G Round each number to the nearest whole number.

1  2  3

H What are the following?

1 $\frac{1}{2}$ **of 370**   2 $\frac{2}{3}$ **of £18**   3 $\frac{7}{10}$ **of 1 kg**

I Put these in order with the smallest first.

3.75 m   **5.75 m**   **3.64 m**   **6.09 m**

J Which of these shapes have parallel sides?
Which of these shapes have perpendicular sides?

a 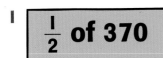   b 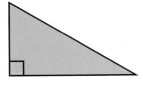   c    d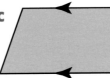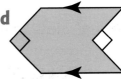

K What is the missing angle?

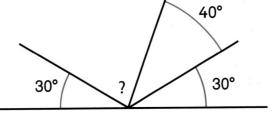

L Estimate the angle.

Measure the angle.

Is it acute or obtuse?

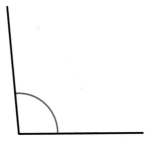

Measuring

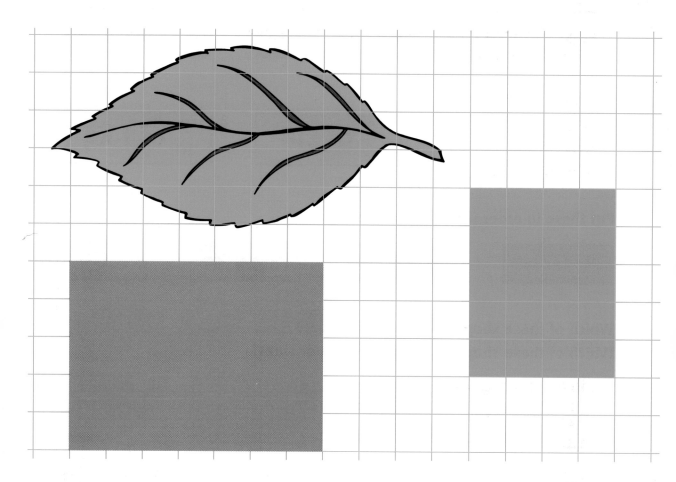

Starters

Look at these shapes.

1 What is the approximate area of the leaf?

2 What is the area of each rectangle?

3 What are the areas of these rectangles?

a 3 cm 5 cm

b 6 cm 5 cm

c 4 cm 4 cm

d 6 cm 3 cm

Practice

A **This graph shows the average weight of someone from birth to age 65.**

1. When were they about 15 kg?
2. When were they about 50 kg?
3. What was their approximate weight when they were 20?
4. What was their approximate weight when they were 35?
5. In which year did they increase in weight the most?

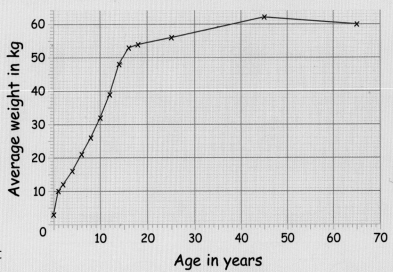

B **Fill in the missing numbers.**

1. $1\frac{1}{2}$ kg = ☐ g
2. $1\frac{3}{4}$ kg = ☐ g
3. $2\frac{1}{4}$ kg = ☐ g
4. 0.4 kg = ☐ g
5. 0.8 kg = ☐ g
6. 0.25 kg = ☐ g
7. 4.2 kg ≈ ☐ kg
8. 3970 g ≈ ☐ kg
9. 1871 g ≈ ☐ kg

C **Try these.**

1. What is half of 3 kg?
2. What is double 1.8 kg?
3. What is a quarter of 3 kg?
4. What is $\frac{1}{10}$ of 5 kg?
5. What is $\frac{1}{100}$ of 7 kg?
6. What is $\frac{1}{100}$ of 3400 g

Challenge

How many marbles weigh 5 kg?

How heavy is a pea?

49

Adding and subtracting

These are number mobiles.

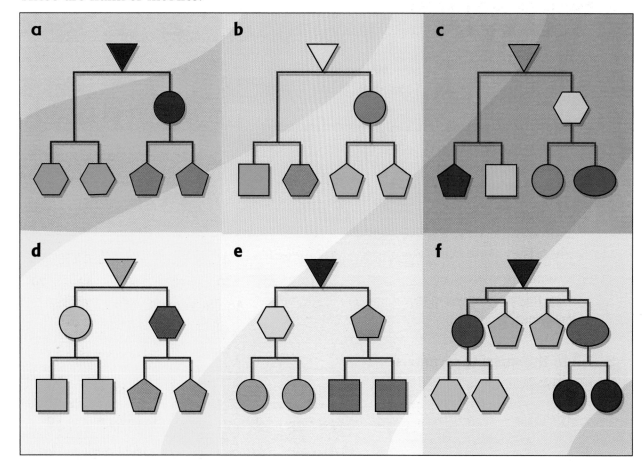

Starters

These are number mobiles.

On each mobile, if the shape is the same then so is the number.

Each side of the mobile must balance.

1 Find ways of balancing when 100 is in each triangle.

2 Choose your own numbers for the triangles.

Make the mobile balance.

Practice

A Answer these in your head.

1 0.7 + 0.9 =	2 1.6 − 0.8 =	3 3.7 + 2.3 =	4 10.0 − 4.8 =
5 346 + 49 =	6 854 − 39 =	7 754 + 31 =	8 680 − 51 =
9 7.2 + 7.3 =	10 1.5 + 1.6 =	11 270 + 280 =	12 715 − 198 =

B Answer the sums. Write three more related facts for each sum.

1 101 − 25 =   2 15.7 + 9.8 =   3 186 + 56 =   4 17.2 − 5.6 =

C Try these.

1 3742	2 6355	3 3958	4 6592	5 3425
+ 646	+ 745	+ 864	+ 879	+ 6247

6 1738	7 2578	8 6324	9 3327	10 2895
+ 5464	+ 8237	+ 2877	+ 6641	+ 5248

D Try these.

1 3.6	2 5.7	3 6.45	4 6.27	5 8.1
+ 8.7	+ 8.6	+ 3.78	+ 3.96	− 5.4

6 9.0	7 6.7	8 9.4	9 3.72	10 5.46
− 3.8	− 5.8	− 3.5	− 1.84	− 3.96

Challenge

Design your own number mobile for 100.

Here is an example.

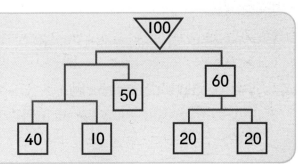

Number problems

a

b

c

d

e

f

g

h

i

Starters

1 Consecutive numbers have been totalled to make each display.

   What could the numbers be?

2 Consecutive numbers have been multiplied to make each display.

   What could the numbers be?

3 Make up division sums for each display.

Practice

A Try these.

1 I think of a number, then divide it by 25. The answer is 30. What was my number?

2 The total of two numbers is 3700. One number is 1577. What is the other?

3 The product of three numbers is 30 000. Two of the numbers are 20 and 30. What is the third number?

4 I am thinking of a number. If I add its double to its half the answer is 20. What is the number?

B How much do these cost?   What is the cost of the following?

1 4 for £5.00   2 10 for £6.50   5 Eight at £1.25 each.   6 Four at 98p each.

3 5 for £7   4 6 for £14.10   7 Six at £4.75 each.   8 Five at £3.99 each.

C Try these.

1 Sanjay saved 75p a week for one year. How much did he save?

2 The total cost of five tickets was £65. How much did one ticket cost?

3 Diesel costs 63.7p a litre. How much will 5 litres cost?

4 Two books cost £7.99 and £4.55. How much change would there be from £20?

D You can use a calculator for these.

1 Frances saves £3.40 each week. How much has she saved after 14 weeks?

2 Leroy saved the same amount each month. After a year he had £148.20. How much did he save each month?

3 How much, to the nearest penny, is £7 divided by 6?

4 How much, to the nearest pound, is £11.36 multiplied by 12?

Challenge

Make up three different word problems to match this division sum.

$\boxed{} \div 38 = 74$

Multiples and factors

99				95			92		90
	77								70
	62						67		
				54					
	41						47		
39						33			30
	21								
19									
0	1	2	3	4					

Starters

Write answers in a sentence.

1 Which multiple of 6 follows 60?

2 Which multiple of 7 comes just before 90?

3 Which multiple of 8 comes nearest to 99?

4 Which multiple of 9 is nearest to 75?

5 What is the largest multiple of both 4 and 5 that can appear on the grid?

Practice

A (42) (28) (54) (64) (49) (81) (18) (36)

1 Write which of these numbers are multiples of 6.

2 Which are multiples of 7?

3 Which are multiples of 9?

4 Which are multiples of 8?

5 Which number is a multiple of both 6 and 7?

6 Which number is a multiple of both 3 and 4?

B Copy and complete each pattern.

1 5   11   17   __   __   __

2 4   11   18   __   __   __

3 6   15   24   __   __   __

4 3   11   19   __   __   __

C Write the missing numbers.

1   3   13   __   __   53   __

2   7   __   15   __   __   27

3   __   19   26   __   40   __

4   17   __   __   44   __   62

D (124) (250) (500) (120) (135) (108) (745) (222)

1 Which number is divisible by 100?

2 Which numbers are divisible by 2?

3 Which numbers are divisible by 4?

4 Which numbers are divisible by 5?

5 Which numbers are divisible by 10?

Challenge

Place numbers on the grid to make it true

(55) (32) (54) (25) (58) (36) (40) (12) (64)

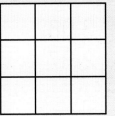

	Multiples of 3	Even number	Divisible by 5
Multiples of 4			
Greater than 50			
Square number			

Review

A What is the area of each shape?

1

12 cm
8 cm

2
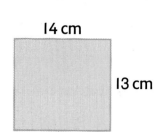
14 cm
13 cm

3
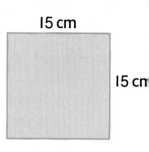
15 cm
15 cm

B How many grams in each of these?

1

$\frac{3}{4}$ kg

2
0.5 kg

3
1.2 kg

C What is the reading on each scale?

1

kg 0   1   2

2
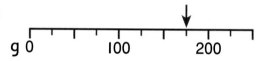
g 0   100   200

D What is the total, in grams, of these?

 $\frac{1}{4}$ kg   200 g   0.75 g   50 g

E Total these.

3842   15   785   9

F Try these.

1
$$\begin{array}{r} 3.08 \\ +\ 2.97 \\ \hline \\ \hline \end{array}$$

2

$$\begin{array}{r} 4.05 \\ -\ 1.78 \\ \hline \\ \hline \end{array}$$

G 1 Which number between 40 and 50 is a multiple of both 6 and 7?

   2 Which number between 130 and 140 is divisible by 9?

   3 Which years between 1990 and 2000 were leap years?

H Try to think of a quick method for these.

1
$$365 + 49$$
2
$$365 - 49$$
3
$$365 \times 49$$

I Say whether the angles are acute, obtuse or right angle.

 1    2   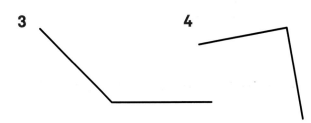 3   4

J Try to answer these in your head.

1
$$40 \times 500$$
2
$$300 \times 8$$
3
$$3000 \div 100$$
4
$$4650 \div 10$$

K Which of the signs <, > or = is missing in each of these?

  1 $(13 \times 2) + (5 \times 4)$ ☐ $7^2 - 3$ **2** $5^2 + 2^2$ ☐ $(30 \times 4) \div 8$

  3 $(86 + 44) - (49 + 27)$ ☐ $(77 - 42) + (55 - 26)$

L Which shapes will fold to make a cube?

1   2 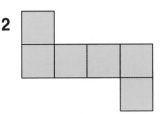   3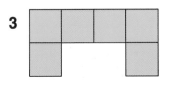

Do you remember?

1 What does this sign mean?

a Is greater than   **b** Is less than

c Is equal to   **d** Is approximately

2 Which is the set of factors for 18?

a 1, 2, 4, 6, 18   **b** 1, 3, 4, 9, 18

c 1, 2, 3, 6, 9, 18   **d** 2, 3, 6, 8, 18

3 Which measurement is the same as 1.2 kg?

a 120 g   **b** 12 000 g   **c** 12 g   **d** 1200 g

4 Which shape has this top view?

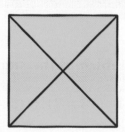

a cuboid   **b** pyramid   **c** cone   **d** prism

5 Name this angle.

a acute   **b** obtuse   **c** right angle

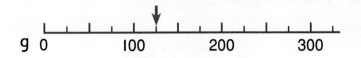

6 **What is the reading?**

g 0   100   200   300

a 150 g   **b** 125 g   **c** 110 g   **d** 120 g

---

7 **What is $\frac{1}{100}$ of 5 kg?**

a 5000 g   **b** 500 g   **c** 50 g   **d** 5 g

---

8 **How many lines of symmetry has this triangle?**

a 0   **b** 1   **c** 2   **d** 3

---

9 **What is the same as 2.05 p.m.?**

a 02:05   **b** 12:05   **c** 14:05   **d** 13:05

---

10 Name this triangle.

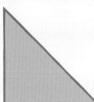

a scalene   **b** isosceles   **c** equilateral

Check your answers on page 96. ✓

Understanding numbers

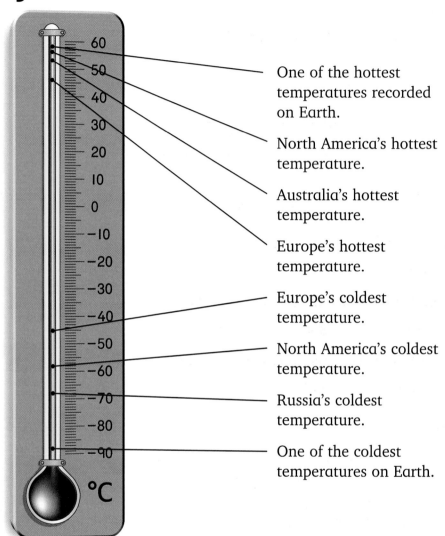

One of the hottest temperatures recorded on Earth.

North America's hottest temperature.

Australia's hottest temperature.

Europe's hottest temperature.

Europe's coldest temperature.

North America's coldest temperature.

Russia's coldest temperature.

One of the coldest temperatures on Earth.

Starters

1 What is one of the hottest recorded temperatures?

2 What is one of the coldest recorded temperatures?

3 What is the difference between these two temperatures?

4 How much hotter is Australia than Europe?

5 How much colder is Russia than Europe?

6 What is the difference between Europe's hottest and coldest temperatures?

Practice

A What number is half-way between these?

  1 1500 and 2000   **2** 3200 and 4000   **3** 6000 and 6900

  4 27 400 and 28 000   **5** 35 470 and 35 480   **6** 24 300 and 24 500

B Estimate the number shown by each arrow.

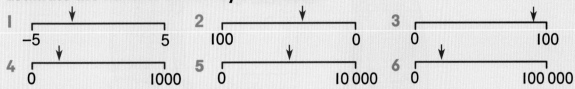

C Round each number to the nearest 10.

  1 436   **2** 2414   **3** 3984   **4** 16 072   **5** 25 955

Round each number to the nearest 100.

  6 783   **7** 3896   **8** 7995   **9** 12 468   **10** 13 246

Round each number to the nearest 1000.

  11 3500   **12** 6712   **13** 9499   **14** 72 386   **15** 59 685

D Try these.

  1 From London to New York is 6799 miles.   **2** A bucket holds 4.2 litres.
     What is this to the nearest 10 miles?   What is this to the nearest litre?

  3 A man weighs 87.4 kg.   **4** How much is £134.25 to the
     What is this to the nearest kilogram?   nearest £10?

  5 There are $365\frac{1}{4}$ days in a year.
     What is this to the nearest day?

Challenge

Work with a friend.

Take turns to enter a 3-digit number into the calculator.

The other person has to reverse the digits in one operation.

**Multiplication
and division**

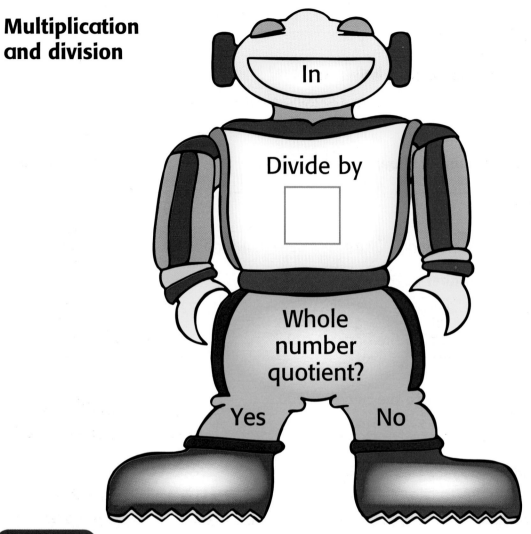

In

Divide by

Whole
number
quotient?

Yes   No

Starters

Divide by 4

In	Quotient and remainder	Fractional quotient	Decimal quotient
9			
26			
39			
83			
121			
258			

Practice

A Answer these as quickly as you can.

1 $11 \times \boxed{} = 77$ 2 $\boxed{} \times 9 = 0.36$ 3 $6 \times \boxed{} = 4.8$ 4 $9 \times \boxed{} = 720$

5 $56 \div \boxed{} = 8$ 6 $\boxed{} \div 8 = 9$ 7 $430 \div 2 = \boxed{}$ 8 $\boxed{} \div 2 = 330$

9 $\boxed{} \div 100 = 4$ 10 $650 \div \boxed{} = 65$ 11 $49 \times 6 = \boxed{}$ 12 $28 \times \boxed{} = 140$

B Try these.

1	2	3	4	5	6
46	56	27	35	74	37
× 37	× 48	× 19	× 54	× 74	× 45

7	8	9	10	11	12
84	27	94	83	26	64
× 76	× 96	× 67	× 46	× 26	× 38

C Try these.

1 £5 ÷ 4 =   2 £6 ÷ 8 =   3 £23 ÷ 5 =   4 £137 ÷ 2 =

5 £14.10 ÷ 6 =   6 £13.65 ÷ 3 =   7 £65.38 ÷ 7 =   8 £52.20 ÷ 9 =

D Write the remainders as fractions.

1 36 ÷ 5 =   2 74 ÷ 9 =   3 68 ÷ 10 =   4 97 ÷ 2 =

5 644 ÷ 8 =   6 144 ÷ 5 =   7 301 ÷ 3 =   8 725 ÷ 7 =

Write the remainder as a decimal.

9 71 ÷ 2 =   10 96 ÷ 5 =   11 59 ÷ 10 =   12 67 ÷ 4 =

13 322 ÷ 8 =   14 344 ÷ 10 =   15 972 ÷ 5 =   16 601 ÷ 4 =

Challenge

Use these digits.

Which arrangement
produces the largest product?

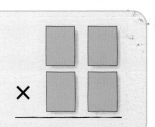

Percentages and problems

20% of children are frightened of the dark

10% off all marked prices
£19
£30

60% of children under the age of 12 still watch TV after 9.00 p.m.

£45

5% of 1 million cars had minor faults !

99% of people wished they were better at maths

Starters

1 What percentage of children are not frightened of the dark?
2 What fraction of children under 12 watch TV after 9 o'clock in the evening?
3 How many cars had minor faults?
4 500 people were asked about maths.
   How many wished they were better at maths?
5 What are the sale prices of the electrical items?

Practice

A How much are these percentages?

1 50% of £3
2 10% of £4
3 70% of £4
4 20% of £8
5 40% of £10
6 30% of £7
7 90% of £20
8 60% of £10
9 1% of £1
10 5% of £1
11 25% of £1
12 75% of £1

B Try these.

1 There is a 50% deposit on a £330 TV. How much is the deposit?

2 Prices are reduced by 25%. How much is taken off a price of £46?

3 10% of a frozen food pack is water. How much water is there in a 1 kg pack?

4 20% is cut from a length of cloth. The cloth was 5 metres long. How much was cut off?

C Try these.

1 I have saved £230. Computer games cost £34. How many can I buy?

2 I have 350 stamps. Each page in my album holds 48 stamps. How many pages do I need?

3 I have 491 stickers. Each page in my album holds 24 stickers. How many complete pages will I have?

4 Each page of stamps has 8 rows and 6 columns. How many stamps are there on 36 pages?

D Try these.

1 What is half of £13.70?

2 Double £13.65.

3 How many lengths of 20 cm can be cut from 370 cm?

4 How many sets of 8 can be made from 145?

5 What is the difference between 34 °C and −5 °C?

6 What is the quotient of 71 divided by 5?

Challenge

Make a '13 stick' with cubes.

Break it into 3 pieces.
The product of the three pieces here is $2 \times 5 \times 6 = 60$.

Investigate the largest product which can be made.

Fractions, decimals and percentages

50%	$\frac{1}{4}$	0.75	$\frac{1}{5}$	70%
0.25	$\frac{7}{10}$	75%	$\frac{1}{2}$	0.2
$\frac{3}{4}$	0.5	0.7	20%	25%
$\frac{4}{5}$	$\frac{3}{100}$	30%	0.8	3%
0.3	0.03	80%	$\frac{3}{10}$	

Starters

Copy and complete the table.

Fraction	$\frac{3}{10}$	$\frac{9}{10}$				$\frac{3}{5}$	
Percentage	30%		40%		15%		85%	
Decimal	0.3			0.1				0.02

Practice

A Calculate these.

1 $\frac{1}{3}$ of 435

2 $\frac{1}{10}$ of 560

3 $\frac{1}{8}$ of 840

4 $\frac{1}{4}$ of 912

5 $\frac{2}{3}$ of 609

6 $\frac{7}{10}$ of 410

7 $\frac{3}{8}$ of 728

8 $\frac{3}{4}$ of 832

9 $\frac{3}{100}$ of 500

10 $\frac{17}{100}$ of 800

11 $\frac{53}{100}$ of 900

12 $\frac{91}{100}$ of 2000

B Write each fraction as a decimal.

1 $\frac{1}{2}$

2 $\frac{3}{4}$

3 $\frac{1}{4}$

4 $\frac{3}{10}$

5 $\frac{7}{10}$

6 $\frac{30}{100}$

7 $\frac{40}{100}$

8 $\frac{7}{100}$

9 $\frac{1}{5}$

10 $\frac{3}{5}$

11 $\frac{4}{5}$

12 $\frac{1}{20}$

C Write each fraction as a percentage.

1 $\frac{1}{2}$

2 $\frac{1}{10}$

3 $\frac{7}{10}$

4 $\frac{9}{10}$

5 $\frac{12}{100}$

6 $\frac{15}{100}$

7 $\frac{1}{4}$

8 $\frac{3}{4}$

9 $\frac{1}{5}$

10 $\frac{3}{5}$

11 $\frac{2}{5}$

12 $\frac{3}{20}$

D Calculate these.

1 10% of 460

2 20% of £300

3 40% of 520 g

4 50% of £150

5 80% of 2300

6 60% of 1000 ml

7 5% of £660

8 1% of 7400

9 2% of 2 kg

Challenge

Make a cube from 8 interlocking cubes.

Investigate ways of breaking it
into identical halves.

Try making larger cubes and
repeating the puzzle.

Ratio and proportion

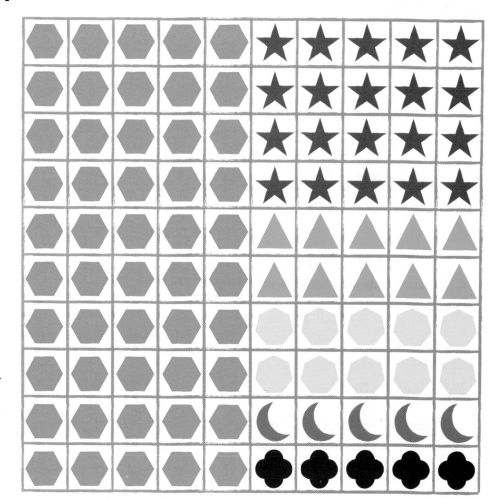

KEY
Biscuits

 chocolate

★ nutty

▲ orange delight

⬡ coconut

☾ raisin dip

✤ cream

1 What proportion of biscuits are chocolate?

2 What proportion of biscuits are coconut?

3 What proportion of biscuits are cream?

4 What percentage of biscuits are nutty?

5 What percentage of biscuits are orange delight?

6 For every 2 biscuits Fran ate, Tony had 3.
If Fran ate 10 biscuits, how many did Tony eat?

Practice

A **Greg has 1 sticker for every 2 that Lisa has.**

Choose the correct word to complete the sentences.

1 Greg has **half/twice** as many as Lisa.

2 Lisa has **half/twice** as many as Greg.

3 Greg has **one third/two thirds** of the stickers.

4 Lisa has **one third/two thirds** of the stickers.

5 If Greg has eight stickers then Lisa has **four/sixteen** stickers.

6 If Lisa has eight stickers then Greg has **four/sixteen** stickers.

B **Try these.**

> Cook 45 minutes for every kilogram. 4 kg

1 How long must the chicken be in the oven?

> **Recipe**
> Add 3 spoons of flour for every $\frac{1}{2}$ litre of milk.

2 How many spoons of flour are needed for $1\frac{1}{2}$ litres of milk?

3 How many litres for 12 spoons of flour?

> **Mixing instructions** For every 2 spoons of mixture add 3 cups of water.

4 How many spoons of mixture are needed for 15 cups of water?

5 How many cups of water are needed for 10 spoons of mixture?

C **Change this recipe for 4 people into one for 6 people.**

> 240 g flour   300 ml milk
> 2 eggs   30 g butter

Challenge

Investigate a set of dominoes.

How many in a complete set?

What proportion have odd totals?

Which totals can only be made one way?

Handling data

Here is a tables test.

6 × 9	8 × 8	5 × 7	4 × 8	6 × 6	4 × 9	4 × 4	7 × 9
7 × 3	5 × 4	2 × 7	7 × 10	4 × 7	3 × 6	5 × 5	10 × 8
8 × 5	4 × 6	5 × 10	9 × 8	2 × 3	6 × 8	3 × 10	9 × 2
5 × 3	3 × 3	2 × 6	4 × 10	5 × 2	2 × 8	7 × 7	6 × 5
3 × 8	9 × 5	2 × 4	8 × 7	7 × 6	3 × 9	3 × 4	9 × 9

Here are some results.

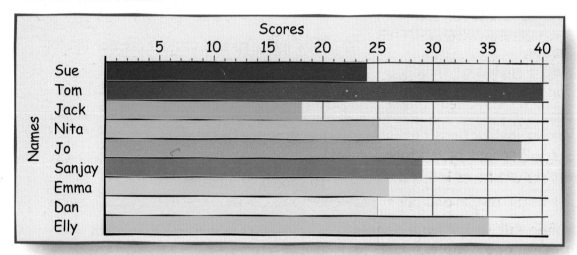

Starters

1 Which score occurred most often?

2 What was the range of marks?

3 Who scored more than Elly?

4 What was the difference between the highest and the lowest scores?

5 Who scored less than half marks?

6 How would you have scored on the test?

Practice

A What is the mode and range for each set of data?

1 36 cm, 42 cm, 49 cm, 36 cm, 41 cm, 56 cm, 36 cm, 42 cm

2 £56, £72, £30, £48, £31, £32, £25, £30

3 450 g, 300 g, 750 g, 750 g, 400 g, 150 g, 750 g, 700 g

4 3.5 kg, 2.5 kg, 1.5 kg, 6.0 kg, 2.5 kg, 2.0 kg, 6.0 kg, 1.0 kg

B Look at these temperature charts.

Temperature charts for 1995 and 1996

1 What was the highest temperature on 1 April 1995?

2 What was the highest temperature on 1 April 1996?

3 At what time did the temperature drop in 1995?

4 At what time did the temperature drop in 1996?

5 When did the temperature exceed 19 °C?

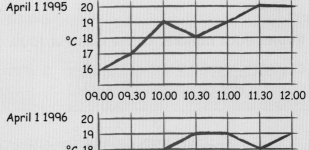

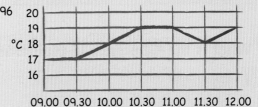

C Class 5 did an experiment to find the number of plants in an area of field.

Look at the results and answer the questions.

1 Which plant grew most widely?

2 Which plant was least common?

3 Do you think it was a large area or a small area?

4 What else can you work out from the graph?

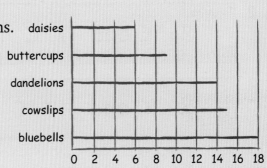

Challenge

Which is the most common shoe size in your class?

Review

A Round each number to the nearest 10.

1 375   2 4226   3 1562   4 3719

B Round each number to the nearest 100.

1 777   2 7340   3 1150   4 23 270

C Round each number to the nearest 1000.

1 7500   2 16 700   3 28 225   4 236 400

D What is the difference in temperature between these?

1 −5 °C and 17 °C

2 24 °C and −7 °C

3 −20 °C and −17 °C

E Write the quotient as a mixed number.

1 71 ÷ 4   2 94 ÷ 4   3 81 ÷ 4

F Write three related facts for this sum.

$$2.1 \div 3 = 0.7$$

G Answer these.

1
$$\begin{array}{r} 34 \\ \times\ 72 \\ \hline \end{array}$$

2
$$\begin{array}{r} 58 \\ \times\ 26 \\ \hline \end{array}$$

3
$$\begin{array}{r} 74 \\ \times\ 39 \\ \hline \end{array}$$

H Write each decimal as a fraction.

1 **0.5**　　2 **0.75**　　3 **0.1**　　4 **0.4**

I Write each fraction as a percentage.

1 $\dfrac{1}{10}$　　2 $\dfrac{30}{100}$　　3 $\dfrac{3}{4}$　　4 $\dfrac{1}{5}$

J Here are the results of rolling a dice 8 times.

What is the mode?

Reflections and symmetry

Here is a tile.

These patterns were made from the tile.

a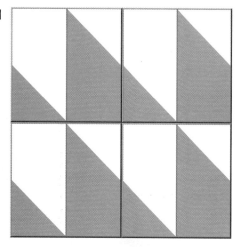

b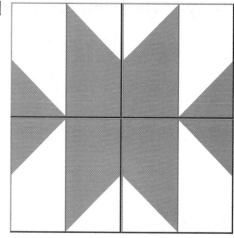

c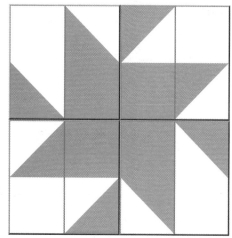

d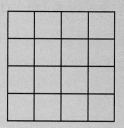

Starters

1 Describe how each pattern is made from the tile.
2 Which of the patterns have lines of symmetry?
3 Design your own tile on a square grid like this.
4 Make patterns using your tile.

Practice

A Copy the grid and shape.
Draw the reflections
of the shape in the
other quadrants.

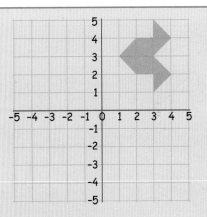

B Sketch each shape and mirror line. Draw the reflections.

1

2

3
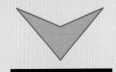

4

C Design a symmetrical pattern on spotty paper.

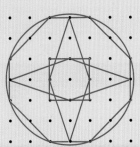
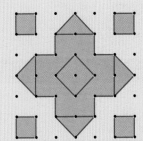

Challenge

Copy this circle pattern.
Design your own circle pattern.

Time

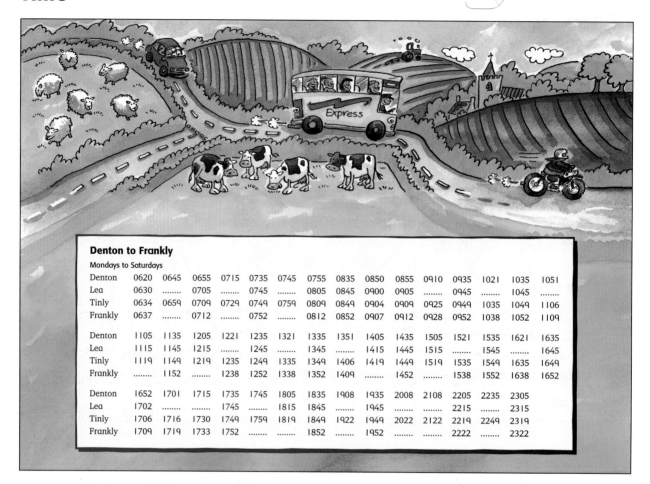

Denton to Frankly

Mondays to Saturdays

Denton	0620	0645	0655	0715	0735	0745	0755	0835	0850	0855	0910	0935	1021	1035	1051
Lea	0630	....	0705	....	0745	....	0805	0845	0900	0905	....	0945	....	1045	....
Tinly	0634	0659	0709	0729	0749	0759	0809	0849	0904	0909	0925	0949	1035	1049	1106
Frankly	0637	....	0712	....	0752	....	0812	0852	0907	0912	0928	0952	1038	1052	1109
Denton	1105	1135	1205	1221	1235	1321	1335	1351	1405	1435	1505	1521	1535	1621	1635
Lea	1115	1145	1215	....	1245	....	1345	....	1415	1445	1515	....	1545	....	1645
Tinly	1119	1149	1219	1235	1249	1335	1349	1406	1419	1449	1519	1535	1549	1635	1649
Frankly	....	1152	....	1238	1252	1338	1352	1409	....	1452	....	1538	1552	1638	1652
Denton	1652	1701	1715	1735	1745	1805	1835	1908	1935	2008	2108	2205	2235	2305	
Lea	1702	....	....	1745	....	1815	1845	....	1945	....	....	2215	....	2315	
Tinly	1706	1716	1730	1749	1759	1819	1849	1922	1949	2022	2122	2219	2249	2319	
Frankly	1709	1719	1733	1752	....	....	1852	....	1952	....	....	2222	....	2322	

Starters

1 How long does it take to travel from Denton to Frankly?

2 How long does it take to travel from Denton to Tinly?

3 How long does it take to travel from Tinly to Frankly?

4 If I catch the 1645 bus from Lea what time will I arrive in Frankly?

5 I must be in Tinly by 4.00 p.m. Which bus should I catch from Denton?

6 I went shopping in Denton.
   I arrived in Denton at 2.00 p.m. and spent $2\frac{1}{2}$ hours there.
   Which bus did I catch home?

Practice

A Complete these time facts.

1 I millenium = ☐ years   2 I century = ☐ years

3 I decade = ☐ years   4 I day = ☐ hour

5 I minute = ☐ seconds   6 I hour = ☐ minutes

B Write these times using either a.m. or p.m.

1	2	3	4	5	6
4:26	15:47	23:59	11:44	13:01	20:11

C Try these.

1 The sponsored walk began at 09.45 and finished at 15.35. How long did it last?

2 A train leaves at 08.05 and arrives at 17.55. How long did the journey last?

3 The sun sets at 20.45 and rises at 05.55. How many hours of darkness?

4 A video is set to start at 19.15 and finish at 21.50. For how long will it be recording?

D Suggest units of time to measure these.

1 The age of an old oak tree.

2 How long it takes a bulb to start growing after it has been planted.

3 How long it is until your birthday.

4 How long a cake will take to bake.

5 How long it takes a cup to fall to the ground.

6 How long you are asleep in a week.

Challenge

Make a time tocker from a lid, card and plasticine.

Try to make a tocker which will rock for 20 seconds.

What affects the number of rocks?

Capacity

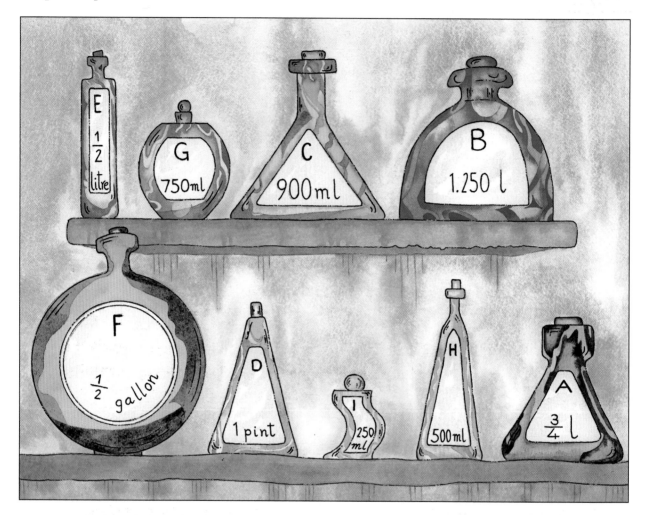

1 Which bottle holds the most?
2 Which bottle holds the least?
3 Which pairs of bottles hold the same?
4 Which bottles hold more than a litre?
5 Which bottles are not metric?

Practice

A **What is the reading on each measuring jug?**

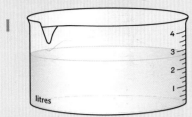

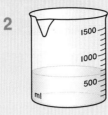

B **Write each measurement as litres.**

1. 5400 ml
2. 1750 ml
3. 2675 ml
4. 3050 ml
5. 3171 ml

Write each measurement as millilitres.

6. 1.5 l
7. 4.25 l
8. 3.75 l
9. 1.05 l
10. 2.375 l

C **Suggest units of measurement to find the capacity of these.**

1. Large bucket
2. Cup
3. Kettle
4. Swimming pool
5. Teaspoon
6. Milk bottle
7. Bath
8. Loch Ness

millilitres	litres
pints	gallons
decilitres	centilitres

D **Try these.**

1. A bottle holds 720 ml. It is $\frac{3}{8}$ full. How much liquid is in the bottle?

2. What is the total capacity of six cans each holding 175 ml?

3. One litre is about $1\frac{3}{4}$ pints. Approximately how many pints are the same as 4 litres?

4. One pint is approximately 0.57 litres. How many litres will be the same as 8 pints?

5. A 750 ml bottle of fruit squash is shared among six people. Approximately how much will each receive?

6. A bottle is holding 0.45 l. How many millilitres must be added to make 1 litre?

Challenge

Old units of capacity included these.

Find out about old units of measuring capacity.

Ka	dram	gill
peck	quart	

Addition and subtraction

2.06	**12.58**	**8.15**
7 8 9 ×	7 8 9 ×	7 8 9 ×
30.55	**1.94**	**77.4**
7 8 9 ×	7 8 9 ×	7 8 9 ×
9.2	**6.93**	**3.45**
7 8 9 ×	7 8 9 ×	7 8 9 ×
5.55	**3.8**	**9.6**
7 8 9 ×	7 8 9 ×	7 8 9 ×

Starters

1 Which pairs when added will give whole number totals?

2 Which numbers will be whole numbers when multiplied by 10?

3 Which pair will be more than 100 when totalled?

4 Which pair will give an answer nearest to 7 when subtracted?

5 Choose any of the numbers to be an answer.
Write 5 different sums to match your answer.

Practice

A Total each set of numbers.

1   43, 596, 8, 3166

2   3425 ml, 25 ml, 175 ml

3   £314, £96, £7, £1216

4   426 cm, 8 cm, 4162 cm

5   4 cm, 1.5 m, 120 cm

6   1.25 kg, 750 g, 3 kg

7   5 ml, 1.25 l, 960 ml

8   5 ml, 5 cl, 5 dl

B Try these.

1	2	3	4	5
3425 + 1964	6835 + 2567	7462 + 3514	6030 – 1479	3857 – 2964

6	7	8	9	10
8314 – 1968	5503 – 1786	3.74 + 6.88	9.06 + 4.94	16.35 + 24.28

11	12	13	14	15
27.64 + 38.44	7.05 – 3.77	6.40 – 3.77	26.08 – 9.69	35.54 – 16.82

C Try these.

1   I buy three items which cost £1.35, £4.99 and £5.85. How much change do I receive from a £20 note?

2   A CD which costs £10.50 is reduced by 50%. What is its new price?

3   I share £126 between Paul and Ben. I give Paul twice as much as Ben. How much will each receive?

4   I buy two books at £7.99 each and three magazines at £2.99 each. How much change do I receive from two £20 notes?

Challenge

Use a calculator to help find the missing digits.

 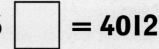 $\boxed{}\boxed{} \times 6\boxed{} = 4012$

81

Properties of numbers

174	**414**	**206**	**382**
483	**331**	**239**	**173**
230	**275**	**170**	**325**
117	**81**	**138**	**262**

Starters

Choose any four numbers from the grid.

Total them.

Find different ways of reaching 100.

Practice

A Which numbers, less than 100, have these as some of their factors?

1 [2, 3, 4, 6, 9, 12, 18]   2 [2, 3, 4, 6, 8, 12]   3 [2, 17]

4 [2, 3, 5, 6, 10, 15]   5 [2, 19]   6 [2, 3, 6, 9, 18]

B Explain, in words, the rule for each sequence.

1 3, 6, 9, 12, 15, ...   2 4, 7, 10, 13, 16, ...

3 1, 4, 9, 16, 25, ...   4 1, 10, 100, 1000, 10 000, ...

5 3, –1, –5, –9, –13, ...   6 81, 72, 63, 54, 45, ...

C Try these.

1 Start with 1. Follow the rule 'triple the previous number then add 1' Write the next six numbers in the sequence.

2 Start with 2 and 3. Follow the rule 'add the previous two numbers together'. Write the next six numbers in the sequence.

3 Start with 16. Follow the rule 'halve the previous number'. Write the next six numbers in the sequence.

D Write rules for what happens when you do these.

1 Add two odd numbers.   2 Add two even numbers.

3 Multiply two odd numbers.   4 Multiply two even numbers.

5 Add an odd and an even number.   6 Multiply an odd and an even number.

Challenge

52, 53 and 54 are consecutive numbers.

Investigate numbers which can be made by totalling consecutive odd numbers.

Review

A Talk about lines of symmetry in these polygons.

1   2   3   4

B Talk about how the triangle has moved each time.

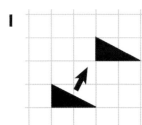 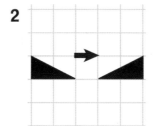 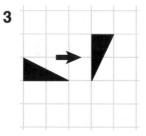

1   2   3

C Copy and draw each reflection.

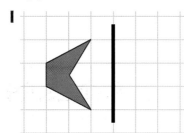 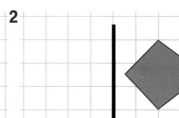 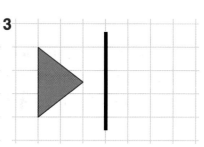

1   2   3

D Talk about these two times.

1    2

E Talk about these containers.

1    2 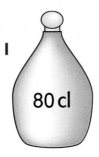   3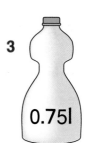

80 cl

725 ml

0.75l

F Total these measures.

$\frac{3}{4}$ **litre**   **600 millilitres**   **1.25 litres**

G Total these numbers.

5   **3472**   **89**

H What do these percentages mean?

1 **10%**   2 **50%**   3 **25%**

I Talk about the factors of these numbers.

1 **81**   2 **36**   3 **100**

J Talk about quick methods for answering these.

1 **3974 + 999 =**   2 **56 × 19 =**   3 **19 @ £3.99**

K Which of these was a leap year?

1564 The birth of William Shakespeare   1666 Great Fire of London   1963 Valentina Tereshkova first woman in space

L Make up word problems for these sums.

1 342 + ☐ = 500   2 ☐ − 724 = 844

Place value

Digits

There are ten digits

0, 1, 2, 3, 4, 5, 6, 7, 8, 9

4-digit numbers

All the whole numbers from 1000 to 9999

thousands   hundreds   tens   units

4   1   6   3

4000 + 100 + 60 + 3

Multiplying and dividing by 10 and 100

Multiplying by 10:
move the digits 1 place to the left and fill the space with a zero.

Multiplying by 100:
move the digits 2 places to the left and fill the spaces with two zeros.

Dividing by 10:
move the digits 1 place to the right.

Dividing by 100:
move the digits 2 places to the right.

Rounding

To the nearest 10:
look at the last digit, if less than 5 round down, otherwise round up

examples
83 round down 80
708 round up 710
1235 round up 1240

To the nearest 100:
look at last two digits, if less than 50 round down, otherwise round up

examples
742 round down 700
1670 round up 1700
27 450 round up 27 500

To the nearest 1000:
look at the last 3 digits, if less than 500 round down, otherwise round up

examples
62 489 round down 62 000
4870 round up 5000
13 500 round up 14 000

Thousands

million	hundred thousands	ten thousands	thousands	hundreds	tens	units

A shorthand way of writing a thousand is to use k:

examples
3000 = 3k
50 000 = 50k

Commas are sometimes used to separate thousands from hundreds:

examples
3425   86,205   159,238

Number patterns

The multiples of 3 are	3, 6, 9, 12, 15, ...
The multiples of 4 are	4, 8, 12, 16, 20, 24, ...
Multiples of 2 are always even	2, 14, 16, 28, 30, 62, ...
Multiples of 5 always end in 5 or 0	15, 40, 65, 80, ...
Multiples of 10 always end in 0	10, 30, 140, 200, ...

Whole numbers are divisible by:

10 if the last digit is 0	350, 2900, 6730, 2190, ...
5 if the last digit is 0 or 5	455, 260, 385, 205, ...
2 if the last digit is an even number	244, 8776, 3108, 2330
3 if the sum of the digits is divisible by 3	81, 162, 255, 834, ...
4 if the last two digits are divisible by 4	144, 1328, 3640, 2076, ...
6 if it is even and also divisible by 3	126, 384, 1056, 3348, ...
8 if half of it is divisible by 4	144, 576, 440, 984, ...
9 if the sum of the digits is divisible by 9	324, 2052, 5787, 2907, ...

Factors are numbers which will divide exactly into other numbers.
The factors of 18 are 1, 2, 3, 6, 9 and 18
The factors of 30 are 1, 3, 5, 6, 10 and 30
5 is a factor of 5, 10, 15, 20, ...
7 is a factor of 7, 14, 21, 28, ...

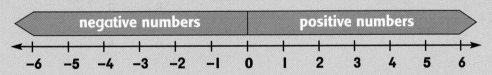

Numbers which can only be divided by themselves and 1.
Prime numbers up to 20 are
2, 3, 5, 7, 11, 13, 17, 19

When looking for a pattern in a sequence of numbers, look at the difference between consecutive numbers:

| 7 | | 11 | | 15 | | 19 | | ... |
| | 4 | | 4 | | 4 | | 4 | |

To make a square number, multiply a number by itself:
$3 \times 3 = 9$
9 is a square number
$7 \times 7 = 49$
49 is a square number

To find the square root of a number, find a number that, when multiplied by itself, gives that number:
$\sqrt{49}$ 7×7 is 49   so $\sqrt{49} = 7$

Addition

Addition can be done in any order

It does not matter in which order you add numbers. Choose the order you find easiest.

examples

$13 + 29 = 29 + 13$

$45 + 93 = 93 + 45$

Knowing doubles

Knowing doubles can help you find other totals.

examples

$50 + 50 = 100$

$51 + 53 = 104$

$46 + 46 = 92$

$46 + 47 = 93$

Addition and subtraction are opposites

An addition sum can be checked by subtracting.

examples

$58 + 46 = 104$

$104 - 46 = 58$

Quick methods

Adding 9:

Add 10 then subtract 1 $74 + 9 = 83$

Adding 19:

Add 20 then subtract 1 $112 + 19 = 131$

Adding 99:

Add 100 then subtract 1 $253 + 99 = 352$

Adding 999:

Add 1000 then subtract 1 $8456 + 999 = 9455$

Adding the tens then the units

When adding TU numbers, try holding the first number in your head and then adding the tens and then the units.

examples

$47 + 36$

$47 + 30 = 77$

$77 + 6 = 83$

Breaking up numbers can help add mentally

4   9 +   3   7   add the tens then
↓   ↓   ↓   ↓   add the units

$(40 + 9) + (30 + 7)$ $70 + 16 = 86$

Adding the nearest decade number and adjusting

$56 + 79$

$56 + [80 \text{ then } -1] = 135$

$64 + 52$

$64 + [50 \text{ then } + 2] = 116$

Subtraction

Quick methods

Subtracting 9:
subtract 10 add 1 $73 - 9 = 64$

Subtracting 19:
subtract 20 add 1 $137 - 19 = 118$

Subtracting 99:
subtract 100 add 1 $481 - 99 = 382$

Difference

To find the difference between two numbers, subtract them.

example
64   97 $97 - 64 = 33$
                                        ↑
                                difference

Subtraction and addition are opposites

A subtraction sum can be checked by adding.

example
$86 - 38 = 48$ $48 + 38 = 86$

Brackets

When brackets are used, work out the sum in the brackets first.
$47 - (4 \times 7)$
       ↑
work out first $47 - 28 = 19$

Subtracting the nearest decade and adjusting

$93 - 48$ $93 - [50$ then $+2] = 45$

$81 - 44$ $81 - [40$ then $-4] = 37$

When subtracting, mentally count on using the 'shopkeepers' method'

$93 - 58$
Count on from 58 to 60
            (hold 2 in your head)
Count on from 60 to 90
            (hold 30 in your head)
Count on from 90 to 93
            (add together 2, 30 and 3)
The answer to $93 - 58$ is 35

When subtracting close numbers, count on or back

$423 - 418$

count on from 418

or count back from 423

The answer is 5

Breaking up numbers can help to subtract mentally

$78 - 46$

$78 - 40 - 6$

$= 38 - 6 = 32$

Multiplication

Multiplying decade numbers

Multiply significant numbers first then adjust for the tens:

multiply first

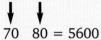

70 80 = 5600

Multiplication and division are opposites

Division is the opposite of multiplication. This can be used to work out missing number problems:

$8 \times ? = 312$

$312 \div 8 = 39$

Multiplying TU numbers by a single digit

Either multiply tens first then units:

58×6

$(50 \times 6) + (8 \times 6)$

$300 + 48 = 348$

or

multiply units first then tens:

$(8 \times 6) + (50 \times 6)$

$48 + 300 = 348$

Approximating answers

Estimate an approximate answer before working out the exact answer, and check that the answer is sensible: 38×63 is approximately 40×60, which is 2400. The exact answer is 2394.

Pencil and paper methods

When a multiplication is too difficult to calculate mentally, use a written method.

```
      37
   ×  49
   ------
     333
    1480
   ------
    1813
```

When calculations are set out in columns, units should line up under units, tens under tens, etc.

Area method

When a multiplication is too difficult to calculate mentally the area method can be used:

68×73

	70	3	
60	4200	180	4380
8	560	24	+ 584
			4964

Halving and doubling

For some calculations, halve the smaller number and double the other:

34×8

68×4

$136 \times 2 = 272$

Division

Dividing by 2: halving

Dividing by 2 is the same as halving:

$72 \div 2 = 36$ half of 72 = 36

Halving odd numbers gives an answer with a half in it:

Half of $85 = 42\frac{1}{2}$ half of $97 = 48\frac{1}{2}$

Remainders

These are the remainders possible when dividing by:

6   0, 1, 2, 3, 4, 5
7   0, 1, 2, 3, 4, 5, 6
8   0, 1, 2, 3, 4, 5, 6, 7
9   0, 1, 2, 3, 4, 5, 6, 7, 8
10   0, 1, 2, 3, 4, 5, 6, 7, 8, 9

Approximating answers

Estimate an approximate answer before working out the exact answer, and check that the answer is sensible:

$612 \div 3$ is approximately $600 \div 3$, which is 200. The exact answer is 204.

Multiplication and division are opposites

Division is the opposite of multiplication. This can be used to work out missing number problems:

$? \div 6 = 42$

$42 \times 6 = 252$

Rules of divisibility

Whole numbers are divisible by:

10 if the last digit is 0
    350, 2900, 6730, 2190, ...

5 if the last digit is 0 or 5
    455, 260, 385, 205, ...

2 if the last digit is an even number
    244, 8776, 3108, 2330, ...

3 if the sum of the digits is divisible by 3
    81, 162, 255, 834, ...

4 if the last two digits are divisible by 4
    144, 1328, 3640, 2076, ...

6 if it is even and also divisible by 3
    126, 384, 1056, 3348, ...

8 if half of it is divisible by 4
    144, 576, 440, 984, ...

9 if the sum of the digits is divisible by 9
    324, 2052, 5787, 2907, ...

Pencil and paper methods

When a division is too difficult to calculate mentally, use a written method.

This method is developed from repeated subtraction.

```
      23
6 ) 138
  - 120    (6 × 20)
    18
    18     (6 × 3)
     0
```

Helpful facts

Fractions

> < = symbols

> means is larger than

< means is smaller than

= means is equal to

$$\frac{1}{3} > \frac{1}{4} \qquad \frac{1}{2} < \frac{3}{4} \qquad \frac{1}{2} = \frac{4}{8}$$

Equivalent strips

Equivalent strips help to compare fractions which are the same.

half

quarter

eighth

half

third

sixth

half

fifth

tenth

Mixed numbers

These are whole numbers and fractions:

$$1\frac{3}{4}, \ 2\frac{1}{3}, \ 4\frac{7}{8}$$

Mixed numbers can be changed to top-heavy fractions (or improper fractions):

$$1\frac{1}{3} = \frac{5}{3} \qquad 2\frac{3}{4} = \frac{11}{4}$$

Denominators and numerators

The denominator shows how many parts the fraction is divided into. The numerator shows how many parts are taken.

$$\frac{1}{2} \quad \begin{array}{l} \leftarrow \text{numerator} \\ \leftarrow \text{denominator} \end{array}$$

Comparing and ordering fractions

When comparing two fractions for size, make the denominators the same and compare the numerators.

Which is larger, $\frac{3}{4}$ or $\frac{5}{8}$?

Make them both eighths:

$$\frac{3}{4} = \frac{6}{8} \text{ so } \frac{6}{8} > \frac{5}{8} \text{ and } \frac{3}{4} > \frac{5}{8}$$

Fractions of quantities

$\frac{1}{2}$ is the same as ÷2 $\qquad$ $\frac{1}{2}$ of 14 = 7

$\frac{1}{5}$ is the same as ÷5 $\qquad$ $\frac{1}{5}$ of 65 = 13

$\frac{1}{10}$ is the same as ÷10 $\qquad$ $\frac{1}{10}$ of 120 = 12

$\frac{1}{3}$ is the same as ÷3 $\qquad$ $\frac{1}{3}$ of 21 = 7

$\frac{1}{4}$ is the same as ÷4 $\qquad$ $\frac{1}{4}$ of 44 = 11

Decimals and percentages

Decimal point

The decimal point separates whole numbers from parts of numbers.

whole number ⟵⟶ part of number

7 . 4

and pounds from pennies

pounds ⟵⟶ pence

£8 . 32

Tenths and hundredths

The decimal point separates whole numbers from parts of numbers.

$\frac{1}{10} = 0.1$ $\frac{3}{10} = 0.3$ $\frac{5}{10} = 0.5$

$\frac{2}{10} = 0.2$ $\frac{3}{4} = 0.75$

tens	units	$\frac{1}{10}$	$\frac{1}{100}$
	7 .	2	
3	4 .	5	8
	8 .	0	6

The decimal point comes between whole numbers and tenths.

whole number ↘ ↙ tenths

6 . 8

Hundredths is that place to the right of the tenths.

$0.42 = \frac{42}{100}$

↗ ↖

4 tenths   2 hundredths

Common fractions and decimals

$\frac{1}{2} = 0.50$ $\frac{1}{10} = 0.1$ $\frac{1}{4} = 0.25$ $\frac{3}{4} = 0.75$

$\frac{1}{3}$ makes a special sort of decimal: it recurs 0333333...

Writing fractions as decimals

Tenths and hundredths can be written as decimals.

$\frac{7}{10} = 0.7$ $\frac{6}{100} = 0.06$ $\frac{35}{100} = 0.35$

Writing decimals as fractions

Decimals can be written as fractions.

$0.3 = \frac{3}{10}$ $0.63 = \frac{63}{100}$ $0.5 = \frac{5}{10} = \frac{1}{2}$

$0.75 = \frac{75}{100} = \frac{3}{4}$

Rounding to the nearest whole

If the decimal is less than $\frac{1}{2}$ or 0.5 round down, otherwise round up.

$3.42 \approx 3.0$ $4.6 \approx 5.0$ $7.5 \approx 8.0$

Per cent sign (%)

A number followed by the per cent sign (%) shows a fraction out of 100.

$35\% = \frac{35}{100}$ $80\% = \frac{80}{100}$

Common percentages

$10\% = \frac{10}{100} = \frac{1}{10}$ $50\% = \frac{50}{100} = \frac{1}{2}$

$25\% = \frac{25}{100} = \frac{1}{4}$ $75\% = \frac{75}{100} = \frac{3}{4}$

$100\% = \frac{100}{100} = 1$ whole

Equivalent fractions

To change from fractions to percentages, make the fraction out of 100.

$\frac{7}{20} = \frac{35}{100} = 35\%$ $\frac{4}{5} = \frac{80}{100} = 80\%$

To change percentages to fractions, make the fraction out of 100 and then simplify the fraction.

$70\% = \frac{70}{100} = \frac{7}{10}$ $45\% = \frac{45}{100} = \frac{9}{20}$

Helpful facts

2-D shapes

Number of sides	Name	Number of sides	Name
3	triangle	7	heptagon
4	quadrilateral	8	octagon
5	pentagon	9	nonagon
6	hexagon	10	decagon

Quadrilaterals

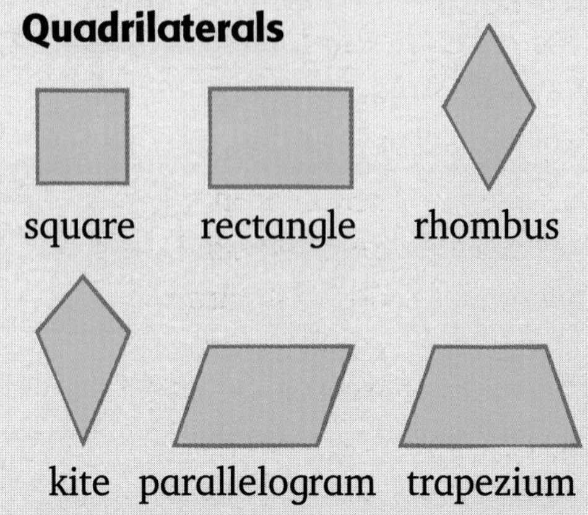

square rectangle rhombus

kite parallelogram trapezium

Triangles

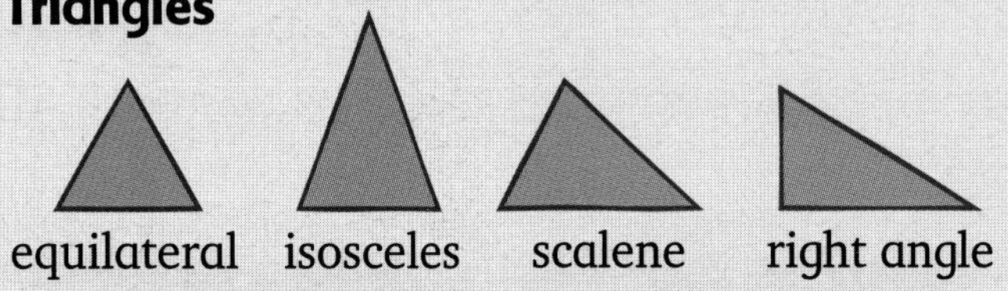

equilateral isosceles scalene right angle

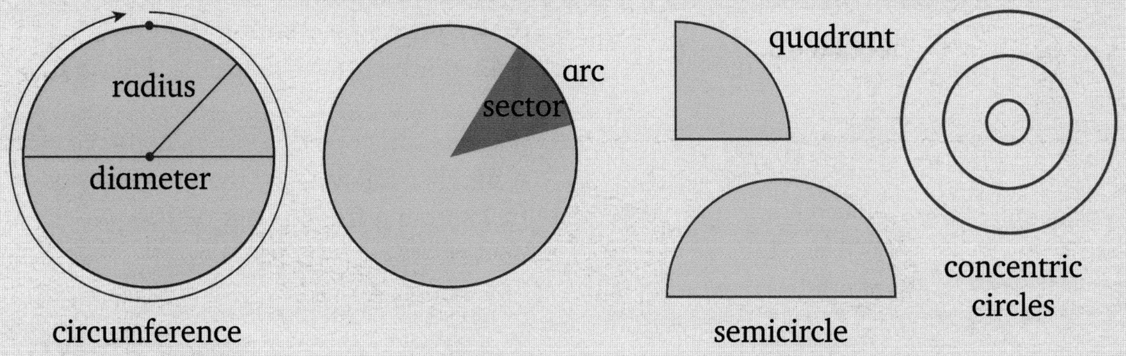

radius
diameter
circumference

arc
sector

quadrant

semicircle

concentric circles

Pentominoes have 5 squares

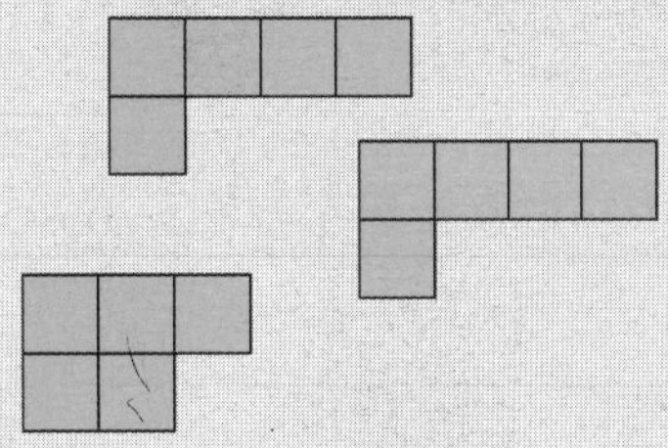

Hexominoes have 6 squares

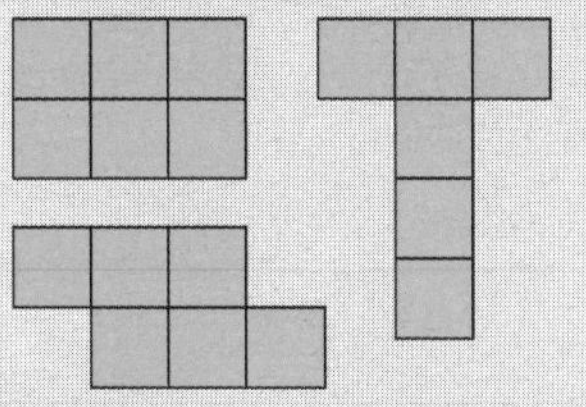

Directions

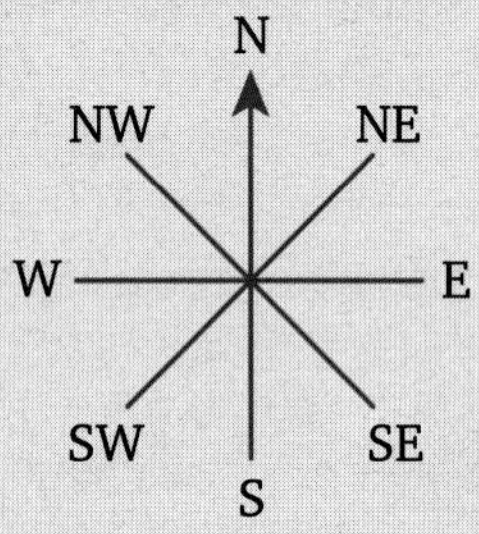

N
NW   NE
W   E
SW   SE
S

parallel lines

perpendicular lines

3-D shapes

Number of faces	Name
4	tetrahedron
6	hexahedron
8	octahedron
10	decahedron
12	dodecahedron
20	icosahedron

Regular solids

There are five regular solids.

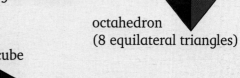

octahedron
(8 equilateral triangles)

hexahedron or cube
(6 squares)

dodecahedron
(12 pentagons)

Net

A net is an opened-out shape.

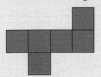 a net of a cube

tetrahedron
(4 equilateral triangles)

icosahedron
(20 equilateral triangles)

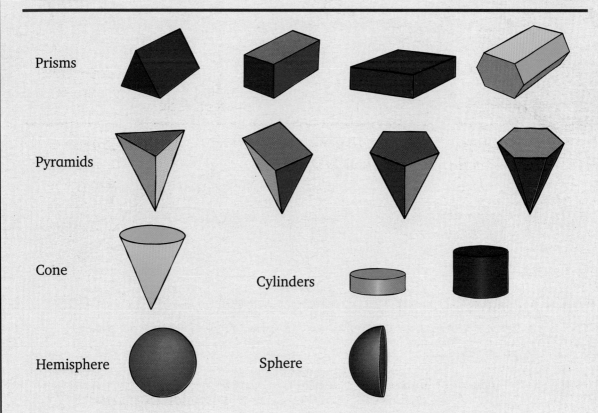

Prisms

Pyramids

Cone

Cylinders

Hemisphere

Sphere

Answers

Do you remember?

Term 1 (pp. 4–5)

1 b	2 b	3 d	4 b	5 d
6 a	7 c	8 b	9 b	10 d

Term 2 (pp. 32–33)

1 c	2 b	3 a	4 d	5 c
6 b	7 a	8 b	9 c	10 c

Term 3 (pp. 58–59)

1 a	2 c	3 d	4 b	5 b
6 b	7 c	8 b	9 c	10 b